Exporting your finished movie

After you finish editing your movie, Adobe Premiere Elements offers several ways for you to enjoy it and share it with friends and family. You can create a DVD for playback on any standard DVD player, you can record it to videotape, or you can export it to a format for the web, e-mail, or other devices or applications.

Burning your movie to DVD

In Adobe Premiere Elements, click Create DVD on the task bar, and select a theme-based template.

Insert a blank DVD disc into a DVD recordable drive.

Click Burn DVD, choose appropriate settings, and then click Burn DVD to create a DVD.

Recording your movie to VHS videotape

In Adobe Premiere Elements, click Export and select To Tape. Insert a tape you can record to in your VCR and set the camcorder to VTR mode. Press Record on your VCR.

You'll need your DV camcorder or an AV-DV converter (an external box) as a bridge between the computer and the VCR.

The AV cable from your camcorder (single connector) connects to the VCR (3 RCA jacks)

audio   video
Composite video

Note: If your DV camcorder doesn't support DV pass-through and you don't have an AV-DV converter, you can copy your movie to a DV tape. Then connect the camcorder to the VCR using the DV camcorder's AV connector jack and cables. Press Play on the camcorder and press Record on the VCR.

Exporting your movie for the web, e-mail, or other devices and applications.

In Adobe Premiere Elements, click Export and select a format appropriate for the destination. For example, select Windows Media for Windows users, QuickTime for Mac OS users, Adobe Flash Video, Others for FLV, iPod and PSP users.

D1308998

Getting started

The first step to creating your movie is to capture or transfer media to your computer. Adobe Premiere Elements makes this simple. The equipment you need depends on the source of the media, as shown below.

Adobe
Premiere
Elements 3.0

DV camcorder[1], HDV camcorder, or webcam

IEEE 1394 (also called FireWire or i.Link) cable[2]

Computer to which you want to capture the media

DVD disc[3]

Computer to which you want to capture the media, equipped with a DVD-ROM or DVD recordable drive[4]

Digital camera, mobile phone, tapeless camcorder, or card reader

USB cable that connects the device to a computer

Computer to which you want to transfer the media

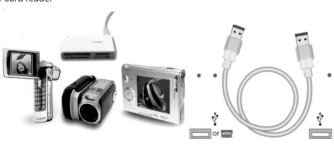

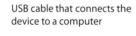
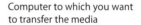

---

1 - To capture footage from analog devices (VCRs, VHS-C or Hi8 camcorders), first make an analog cable connection to an AV-DV converter or a DV camcorder that supports AV-DV pass through. Then connect the converter or DV camcorder to your computer via the IEEE 1394 connector.

2 - Or USB cable if your camcorder or webcam supports DV via USB2, sometimes called USB Video Class 1.0.

3 - DVD camcorders require that you finalize a DVD disc before removing it from the camcorder. You can also transfer media from other kinds of DVD discs, such as set-top DVD recorder discs. Motion-picture CSS-protected DVDs are not supported.

4 - The disc will not be readable in a CD-only drive.

Adobe

Adobe®
Premiere® Elements 3.0

WINDOWS® XP

Adobe®

Contents

Chapter 1: Getting started

Installation and registration. 1

Adobe Help Center 2

Using Help 3

Tips and training 6

New features. 8

Chapter 2: Tutorials

Learn the Adobe Premiere Elements workflow. 11

Tutorial 1: Organize, arrange, and edit clips 12

Tutorial 2: Add effects, transitions, and a soundtrack 18

Tutorial 3: Add a title 24

Tutorial 4: Create a DVD. 28

Tutorial 5: Capture video into a new project 35

Chapter 3: Projects and workspaces

Project basics 39

Project settings and presets. 41

Workspaces and panels. 43

Undoing and saving changes 47

Working with scratch disks. . . . . ❷

Chapter 4: Adding media

Adding media basics 51

Setting up for capturing 52

Capturing video. 56

Adding files to a project 66

Keeping track of clips and source files 75

❷ Indicates a topic that appears only in Help

Creating specialty clips . . . . ❓

Analyzing clip properties and data rate. . . . . ❓

Working with aspect ratios. . . . . ❓

Working with square-pixel footage. . . . . ❓

Working with offline files . . . . ❓

Chapter 5: Arranging clips

Arranging basics 79

Arranging clips in the Sceneline. 81

Understanding the Timeline 88

Working with tracks in the Timeline . . . . ❓

Arranging clips in the Timeline. . . . . ❓

Grouping, linking, and disabling clips . . . . ❓

Working with clip and timeline markers . . . . ❓

Previewing movies 93

Chapter 6: Editing clips

Clip editing basics 99

Trimming clips in the Preview window 100

Trimming clips in the Sceneline 103

Trimming clips in the Timeline 105

Splitting clips 109

Retrieving trimmed frames 111

Changing clip speed, duration, and direction. 113

Freezing and holding frames. 115

Working with source clips . . . . ❓

Editing clips in their original applications. . . . . ❓

Chapter 7: Applying transitions

Transition basics. 119

Applying transitions 121

Adjusting transitions 128

Chapter 8: Applying effects

Effects basics. 131

Finding and organizing effects. 132

Applying and removing effects 134

❓ Indicates a topic that appears only in Help

Working with effect presets. 138

Adjusting effects 139

Superimposing and transparency. . . . . ❓

Selecting colors for effects and mattes . . . . ❓

Chapter 9: Animating effects

Effect animation basics 143

Displaying, adding, and removing keyframes. 145

Adjusting keyframes. 148

Controlling change between keyframes. . . . . ❓

Animating a clip's position . . . . ❓

Effects reference

Adjust. . . . . ❓

Blur and sharpen . . . . ❓

Channel. . . . . ❓

Distort . . . . ❓

GPU. . . . . ❓

Image control . . . . ❓

Keying . . . . ❓

Perspective . . . . ❓

Pixelate . . . . ❓

Render. . . . . ❓

Stylize . . . . ❓

Time . . . . ❓

Transform . . . . ❓

Gallery of video effects . . . . ❓

Audio effects. . . . . ❓

Chapter 10: Creating titles

Creating and trimming titles 151

Creating titles from templates 155

Designing titles for TV 156

Editing and formatting text 158

Applying styles to text and graphics 162

Adding shapes and images to titles 164

Arranging objects in titles 166
Adding color and shadows 170
Creating rolls and crawls. 174
Exporting and importing titles 176

Chapter 11: Adding and mixing audio

Audio basics 179
Adding narrations and soundtracks 179
Mixing audio 183

Chapter 12: Creating DVDs

DVD basics. 187
Working with DVD markers 188
Creating DVDs without menus 198
Creating DVDs with menus 198
Previewing DVDs. 207
Burning DVDs 208

Chapter 13: Exporting and archiving

Exporting basics. 215
Exporting for hard disk playback 217
Exporting for the web and mobile devices. 220
Exporting to videotape 224
Exporting to Video CDs 228
Archiving projects 229

Chapter 14: Using Adobe Photoshop Elements with Adobe Premiere Elements

Using both products together 233
Getting files from Photoshop Elements. 234
Enhancing slide shows with Premiere Elements 238
Enhancing videos with Adobe Photoshop Elements 242

Chapter 15: Keyboard shortcuts

Using default shortcuts. 245
Customizing shortcuts. 245

❓ Indicates a topic that appears only in Help

Troubleshooting

Resources and guidelines .... ❓

Capturing .... ❓

Importing .... ❓

Playing back and previewing .... ❓

Creating a DVD .... ❓

Glossary

Index 247

Chapter 1: Getting started

Installation and registration

To install

1 Close any applications that are open.

2 Insert the product disc into your computer's disc drive.

3 After the Autoplay screen appears, follow the on-screen instructions.

Note: If the Autoplay screen doesn't appear, double-click My Computer, double-click the product disc icon, and then double-click the Setup.exe file.

For more detailed instructions about installing the software and installing an upgrade, see the How To Install file on the product disc. For a list of system requirements, see the product page on the Adobe website. For details about the permitted number of computers on which you can install the software, see the license agreement included with the software.

To register

Register your Adobe® product to receive support on installation and product defects and notifications about product updates.

❖ Do one of the following:

• Install the software to access the Registration dialog box, and then follow the on-screen instructions. An active Internet connection is required.

• Register at any time by choosing Help > Registration.

Adobe Help Center

About Adobe Help Center

Adobe® Help Center is a free, downloadable application that includes two primary features.

Product Help Provides Help for Adobe desktop products installed on your system. (If no Adobe desktop products are installed, topics for them aren't available.) Help topics are updated periodically and can be downloaded through Adobe Help Center preferences. For the products you've installed, Product Help also provides dynamic listings of the top support issues and the most recent support documents published on Adobe.com.

More Resources Provides easy access to the extensive resources on Adobe.com, including support pages, user forums, tips and tutorials, and training.

To check for updates

Adobe periodically provides updates to software and to topics in Adobe Help Center. You can easily obtain these updates through Adobe Help Center. An active Internet connection is required.

1 In the top-right corner of Adobe Help Center, click the Preferences button ⬚ .

2 In the Preferences dialog box, click Check For Updates. If updates are available, follow the on-screen directions to download and save them.

You can also check for updates from within many Adobe applications by choosing Help > Updates.

To set Adobe Help Center preferences

1 In the top-right corner of Adobe Help Center, click the Preferences button ⬚ .

2 Set any of the following options, and click OK.

User Interface Language Specifies the language in which Adobe Help Center interface text is displayed.

Check For Updates Searches for new updates to software and Help topics as they become available from Adobe. This option also lets you specify notification options and choose which applications to update.

To view support documents

From within Adobe Help Center, you can get up-to-the-minute listings of the top support issues and the most recent documents added to the support knowledgebase. Each time you start Adobe Help Center, it uses RSS (Really Simple Syndication) technology to gather this information from the Adobe website and update the listings dynamically.

1 In Adobe Help Center, select a product from the Product Help For menu.

2 Click the Contents tab in the navigation pane, and do either of the following:

• Click Recent Support Documents to display a summary of the most recent documents for the selected product.

• Click Top Issues to display a summary of the top issues documents for the selected product.

3 To view a document in full on the Adobe website, click its link. (An active Internet connection is required.)

To display More Resources

The More Resources section in Adobe Help Center provides easy access to some of the content and services available from the Adobe website, including support, training, tutorials, and forums.

❖ To display this section, click the More Resources button  .

Using Help

Using Help

The complete documentation for using your Adobe product is available in Help, a browser-based system you can access through Adobe Help Center. Help topics are updated periodically, so you can always be sure to have the most recent information available. For details, search for "check for updates" in Help.

Important: Adobe Help systems include all of the information in the printed user guides, plus additional information not included in print. A PDF version of the complete Help content, optimized for printing, is also provided on the product disc.

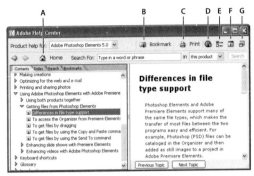

Product Help section of Adobe Help Center
A. Returns you to Help home page **B.** *Adds bookmark for current topic* **C.** *Prints contents of right pane*
D. *More resources* **E.** *Opens Preferences dialog box* **F.** *Opens About Adobe Help Center window* **G.** *Compact view*

To navigate Help

❖ Do any of the following:

- To view Help for a product, choose the product name from the Product Help For menu.

- To expand or collapse a section, click the blue triangle ▶ to the left of the section name.

- To display a topic, click its title. (Topics are identified by a page icon 🔲.)

To search Help topics

Search using words or phrases to quickly find topics. You can search Help for one product or for all Adobe products you've installed. If you find a topic that you may want to view again, bookmark it for quick retrieval.

1 In Adobe Help Center, choose a product from the Product Help For menu.

2 Type one or more words in the Search For box, and choose an option from the In menu:

This Product Searches Help for the selected product.

All Products Searches Help for all Adobe products you have installed.

Search Help for one product or for all products you've installed

3 Click Search. Topics matching the search words appear in the navigation pane, grouped by product and listed in order of relevance.

4 To view a topic, click its title.

5 To return to the Contents tab, do one of the following:

• Click the Home button.

• Click the Back button.

• Click Next Topic or Previous Topic.

Search tips

The search feature in Adobe Help Center works by searching the entire Help text for topics that contain any of the words typed in the Search For box. These tips can help you improve your search results in Help:

• If you search using a phrase, such as "shape tool," put quotation marks around the phrase. The search returns only those topics containing all words in the phrase.

• Make sure that the search terms are spelled correctly.

• If a search term doesn't yield results, try using a synonym, such as "web" instead of "Internet."

To print a topic from Help

1 Select the topic you want to print, and click the Print button.

2 Choose the printer you'd like to use, and then click Print.

To change the view

By default, Adobe Help Center opens in Full view. Full view gives you access to the Product Help and More Resources sections. Switch to Compact view when you want to see only the selected Help topic and you want to keep the Help window on top of your product workspace.

❖ Click the view icon ▭ to switch between Full and Compact views.

To use bookmarks

You can bookmark especially helpful topics for easy access, just as you bookmark pages in a web browser.

- To view bookmarks, click the Bookmarks tab in the navigation pane.

- To create a bookmark, select the topic you want to mark, and click the Bookmark button ▤. When the New Bookmark dialog box appears, type a new name in the text box if desired, and then click OK.

- To delete a bookmark, select it in the Bookmarks tab, and click the Delete button 🗑 . Click Yes to confirm the deletion.

- To rename a bookmark, select it in the Bookmarks tab, and then click the Rename Bookmark button ▭. In the dialog box, type a new name for the bookmark and then click OK.

- To move a bookmark, select it in the Bookmarks tab, and then click the Move Up button ⬆ or the Move Down button ⬇ .

Tips and training

Learning resources

Adobe provides a wide range of resources to help you learn and use Adobe products.

- Tutorials: Short step-by-step lessons that guide you through workflows to produce end results and help you learn the software.

- How Tos: A collection of quick procedures to help you complete common tasks.

- Support: Complimentary and paid technical support options from Adobe.

- Other resources: Training, books, user forums, product certification, and more.

- Extras: Downloadable content and software.

Tutorials

The Help system includes several step-by-step tutorials on key features and concepts. These tutorials are also available in the complete, printable, PDF version of Help, included on the product disc.

To use these tutorials with the product, select the tutorial you want from the Contents tab in Adobe Help Center, and click the View icon ▭ to switch to Compact view. Compact view keeps the Help window on top of the application windows, regardless of what window or application is selected. Drag an edge or a corner of the Help window to resize it.

The Adobe website provides additional tutorials that take you beyond the basics, showing you special techniques and ways to produce professional results. You can access these tutorials from the product page on Adobe.com.

How Tos

How Tos are short sets of instructions that help you quickly complete common tasks. Some How Tos also contain links to related topics in Help.

To access How Tos, choose Window > How To, and then select a task set from the pop-up menu.

Other resources

Additional sources of information and help are available for Adobe products.

- Visit the Training area of the Adobe website for access to Adobe Press books; online, video, and instructor-led training resources; Adobe software certification programs; and more.

- Visit the Adobe user forums, where users share tips, ask questions, and find out how others are getting the most out of their software. User forums are available in many languages. See the main Support page of your local Adobe website.

- Visit the Support area of the Adobe website for additional information about free and paid technical support options. Top issues are listed by product on the Adobe U.S. and Adobe Japan websites.

• Click More Resources in Adobe Help Center to access many of the resources on the Adobe website and to create a custom list of user groups, websites, and contacts you frequently turn to for information.

Extras

The Downloads area of the Adobe website includes free updates, tryouts, and other useful software. In addition, the Plug-ins section of the Adobe Store provides access to thousands of plug-ins from third-party developers, helping you automate tasks, customize workflows, create specialized professional effects, and more.

New features

What's new

Get started quickly

Import from virtually any device Easily import video, audio, and still images from virtually any media device, including DV and DVD camcorders, HDV devices, webcams, unprotected DVDs, digital still cameras, MPEG-4 video recorders, mobile phones, and Windows˙ Media Center. (See "To add files from DVDs, still cameras, mobile phones, tapeless camcorders, and other devices" on page 72.)

Enjoy native HDV support Get crisper, deeper, richer results by capturing, editing, and exporting HDV footage in its native format. (See "To capture from DV and HDV camcorders" on page 58.)

Easily create videos and DVDs

Easily build your movie in the visual Sceneline Assemble your video faster in the visual Sceneline in the My Project panel, which lets you quickly drag, drop, and rearrange thumbnails of your clips, transitions, and enhancements. It's as easy as making a photo slide show. (See "Using the Sceneline view of the My Project panel" on page 81.)

Edit right in the Monitor window Edit and view your movie in one convenient place, the Monitor window, where you can drag one scene onto another to create picture-in-picture effects; type titles and other text right on screen; and preview to TV as you go. (See "To trim a clip in the Monitor panel" on page 103.)

Have fun with still-frame animation Try your hand at animation! Use Stop Motion Capture to create your own time-lapse movies, claymations, and other still-frame animations. (See "To set up for stop-motion or time-lapse capture" on page 61.)

Enjoy full-screen previews Preview your movie in full-screen mode with the click of a button. (See "To preview in full-screen mode" on page 96.)

Wow your audience

Narrate your stories Tell the story in your own voice by adding narration to your video. (See "To narrate a clip" on page 180.)

Create a more polished soundtrack Fade music in and out, mix in narration, and adjust levels in real time. (See "About audio mixing" on page 183.)

Share on mobile phones and portable devices Show your finished movies on virtually any portable device—including mobile phones, video iPods·, and Sony Playstation· Portables—by exporting them in MPEG-4 format. (See "About web formats" on page 220.)

Chapter 2: Tutorials

Learn the Adobe Premiere Elements workflow

Get ready to amaze your friends and family! In a few short tutorials, you'll learn to edit footage and stills into Hollywood-style movies and DVDs. You'll arrange the shots, add transitions to move from one scene to the next, apply a special effect, and enter titles. Once you've learned the basics, you'll learn how to capture video from your camera and start editing your own movies.

In addition to these interactive tutorials, check out the overview videos at www.adobe.com/go/pre_tipstricks.

Although each project you work on is unique, the basic workflow in Adobe Premiere Elements includes the following tasks:

1. Capture video and add other media to a project Transferring video from your camcorder is easy in Adobe Premiere Elements. You connect your camcorder to your computer, open the Capture panel, and click Get Video. Then enhance your movies by adding clips, still images, or music from other sources, such as still cameras, CDs and DVDs, mobile phones, and more.

2. Arrange your movie in the Sceneline In the Sceneline of the My Project panel, you arrange video, audio, and still-image clips to create your movie. By default, Adobe Premiere Elements automatically adds captured video clips to the Sceneline. To add other items, drag them from the Media panel.

3. Preview your movie and edit clips in the Monitor panel You preview your work in the Monitor panel, which provides tools that let you trim unwanted footage and split clips. At the click of a button, you can expand the preview to fill the screen and evaluate your movie in perfect detail.

4. Apply effects and transitions Add polish or humor to your movie with effects and transitions. Effects can alter or distort images, produce artistic effects, or correct problems, such as color casts or poor lighting. Transitions let you control how movies shift from one scene to another. Choose from subtle crossfades or dissolves to stylized page turns or spinning pinwheels.

5. Add a title and credits To put the finishing touches on your movie, add a title, credits, and captions. Adobe Premiere Elements includes dozens of title templates grouped by theme for a variety of occasions. All the templates provide text and graphics to quickly get you started.

6. Share your movie Put your movie on the web in QuickTime, MPEG, or Windows Media format. Optimize for mobile phones or video iPods by simply choosing an export preset. Or burn your movie to a DVD, complete with menus that let your viewers navigate to different scenes.

Tutorial 1: Organize, arrange, and edit clips

You can easily organize your video clips into a seamless movie by using the editing tools and effects in Adobe Premiere Elements. This tutorial shows you how to arrange and edit clips and still images by using samples from a family vacation in San Francisco.

1. Look at the finished movie to see what you'll create.

Start Adobe Premiere Elements and click Tutorials on the welcome screen. (If Adobe Premiere Elements is already open, close the current project to return to the welcome screen.) Click the Play button ▶ in the Monitor panel to view the movie that you'll create in these tutorials. Notice that the *current-time indicator* ⊤ moves through the mini-timeline above the Play button as the movie plays.

Below the Monitor panel, where you preview and edit clips, is the My Project panel, where you arrange clips in the order you want them to appear. (The default Sceneline view of the My Project panel makes arranging clips a snap.) In addition to video, still images, and audio, this movie contains a title, some transitions, and special effects.

Now that you've seen the finished movie, it's time to create it yourself.

2. Open the tutorial project.

Choose File > Open Project. Navigate to the following folder: Program Files/Adobe/Adobe Premiere Elements 3.0/Tutorial

Select the tutorial_start.prel file, and click Open. (If prompted to save changes to tutorial_final.prel, click No.)

Choose File > Save As, specify a new name and location for the project, and click OK.

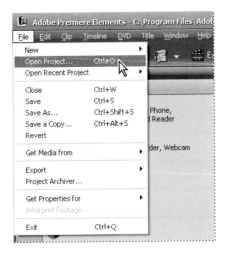

3. Organize your clips.

In the Media panel, click the Available Media button . When you have a lot of clips in a project, it helps to group them into folders. Click the Folder icon at the bottom of the Media panel, and type **Video** into the box. Drag all the video clips into the folder. Create another folder named **Stills** and drag all the still images into it.

To identify video clips, look for the word "Movie" in the Media Type column of the Media panel. To identify still images, look for the words "Still Image."

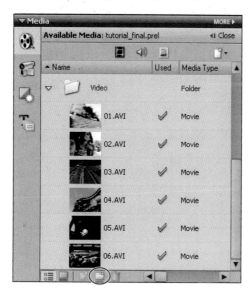

4. Delete unwanted clips.

Click the Play button ▶ in the Monitor panel to view the unedited footage of the family in San Francisco. You'll delete the clip of the children posing in colorful hats, which doesn't fit the trolley and carousel theme. In the Sceneline, select the clip of children posing, and press Delete. The remaining clips shift to fill the gap.

Notice that although you deleted the clip from the Sceneline, it still remains available in the Media panel. In the Used column, the green check mark is removed, indicating that the clip isn't currently in the movie.

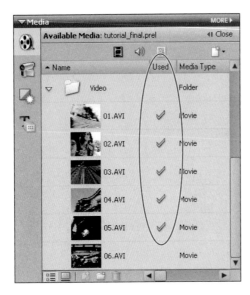

5. Trim a clip.

In the Sceneline, select the clip of the family on the cable car (the second clip). In the Monitor panel's mini-timeline, the clip appears with trim handles on either end. You'll trim this clip to focus on the fun part. In the mini-timeline, drag the In point ▯ slowly to the right until you see the girl and the woman start to wave. Notice that the Monitor panel shows both the clip that you are trimming and the last frame of the adjacent clip.

You needn't worry about carefully trimming clips. Trimming does not delete frames; it sets different In and Out points (also called start and end points). You can retrieve trimmed frames at any time.

6. Create a slide show using still images.

In the Available Media view of the Media panel, double-click the Stills folder. Click the Icon View button ▭ at the bottom of the Media panel. This view allows you to arrange the still images in the order you want for the slide show. (If you can't see all of the images, drag the right side of the panel.) Drag the still image of the woman waving so that it is the last image in the slide show. Press Ctrl+A to select the remaining still images.

Drag the horizontal scroll bar in the Sceneline until you see the first empty clip placeholder. Now drag the still images to the placeholder. From the pop-up menu, choose Add As Grouped Slideshow. In the Create Slideshow dialog box, specify 120 Frames for Image Duration, and then click OK . The slide show appears as a single clip in the Sceneline. To preview it, move the current-time indicator in the Monitor panel to the previous clip ◄ , then press the spacebar.

To save your changes, choose File > Save.

Tutorial 2: Add effects, transitions, and a soundtrack

With Adobe Premiere Elements, you can add special effects, correct color and lighting, and add transitions between scenes. In this tutorial, you'll add an effect and transition to the project you created in "Tutorial 1: Organize, arrange, and edit clips" on page 12. You'll also add a soundtrack.

1. Split a clip.

You can apply an effect to all or part of a clip. To apply an effect to part of a clip, you need to split the clip. In the Sceneline, select the first clip of the carousel (the fourth clip). In the Monitor panel, drag the current-time indicator ⊤, to the middle of the clip (where the words *Pier 39* are centered in the frame). Click the Split Clip button ⊁.

Two instances of clip 04 now appear in the Sceneline. Both instances link to the same video file, but they have unique In and Out points.

2. Apply an effect.

Click the Effects And Transitions button 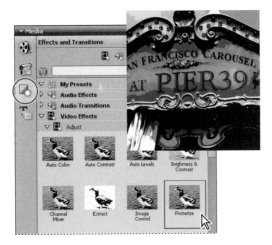 in the Media panel. Expand the Video Effects group, and then expand the Adjust group. Drag the Posterize effect to the clip image in the Monitor panel. To preview the effect, position the current-time indicator before the clip, and click the Play button .

3. Adjust effect properties.

The Properties panel lets you adjust clip settings—such as brightness, contrast, opacity, and rotation—and fine-tune the effects you've applied. Select the second instance of the carousel clip in the Sceneline. Expand the Posterize effect in the Properties panel, and change the Level value to 5. In the Monitor panel, click the Play button to see the change.

To change effects over time, use keyframes. To learn more, see "About keyframes" on page 143.

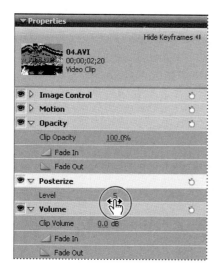

4. Transition between clips.

To give the movie even more visual interest, you'll apply a transition between clips. In the Effects And Transitions view ![icon] of the Media panel, collapse the Video Effects group. Open the Video Transitions group, and then expand the Dissolve group. To animate the thumbnail of a transition, click it. Drag the Additive Dissolve transition to the Sceneline, and place it between the second instance of the carousel clip and the clip of the kids riding the carousel horse.

In the Monitor panel, click the Play button ![icon] to see the transition.

In the Properties panel, you can adjust durations, start points, and end points for transitions. Select Show Actual Sources to see a helpful preview of the adjacent clips.

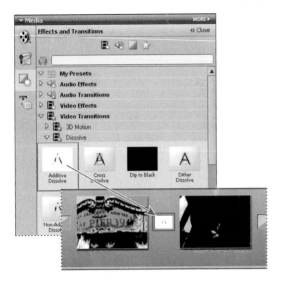

5. Replace the audio.

In the Monitor panel, click the Go To Beginning button. Press the spacebar and listen to the audio of the project. Much of the audio is hard to hear or noisy. You'll replace the audio with some fun music. Click the Available Media button in the Media panel. At the bottom of the panel, click the Up button to close the Stills folder. Drag the fun_music.wav file to the Soundtrack in the Sceneline. To start the music at the beginning of the movie, drag the audio clip all the way to the left.

In the Scenes section of the Sceneline, click the Volume button, and drag the slider all the way down to mute the audio of all the video clips.

Again, click the Go To Beginning button in the Monitor panel, and press the spacebar to listen to the new soundtrack.

6. Fade out music.

In the Sceneline, select the audio clip in the Soundtrack. In the Properties panel, click Fade Out ◣ . To hear the results, click the Go To Beginning button ◄◄ in the Monitor panel, and press the spacebar. Then save the project.

To trim an audio clip in the Soundtrack, move the pointer over the end of the clip, and drag.

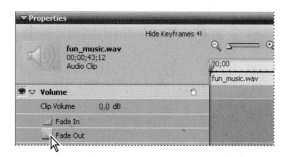

Tutorial 3: Add a title

Titles give your movie a professional look, and captions identify people or places or add commentary. To get you started, Adobe Premiere Elements includes a wide variety of title templates.

1. Select a title template.

Open the project you saved in the previous tutorial. In the Monitor panel, click the Go To Beginning button ◄◄. In the Media panel, click the Title Templates button ⬚. The templates are grouped by theme. Expand the General folder, and then expand the Ocean Waves folder. Drag the oceanwaves_frame template to the clip image in the Monitor panel.

2. Add text to the title.

Double-click the main title. The pointer changes to the Type tool $\mathrm{\underline{I}}$. Drag across the title to select it, and type **San Francisco**. To center the title, click the Pointer tool ➤, select San Francisco, and click Horizontal Center ⬚. You won't need the subtitle, so select it, and press Delete.

 To apply different text styles and fonts, experiment with options in the Properties panel.

3. Change the duration of the title.

In the Monitor panel's mini-timeline, the title appears in purple. Drag the Out point ⬜ to the right until it extends almost to the end of the first clip.

4. Transition from the title to the next scene.

In the Effects And Transitions view  of the Media panel, expand the Video Transitions group, and then expand the Iris group. Drag the Iris Round transition between the first and second clips in the Sceneline. To preview the transition, click the Play button ▶ in the Monitor panel.

5. Render and save the finished movie.

To preview your movie, Adobe Premiere Elements must process all your edits as it displays each frame. If the preview is slow or jerky, it helps to *render* the movie first. Rendering lets Adobe Premiere Elements fully process your edits (trims, effects, titles, soundtracks, and transitions) and save them to a file for faster previewing. Press Enter to render and preview the movie. (For more information about rendering, see "Previewing a movie in the Monitor panel" on page 93.)

Congratulations! You've completely arranged and edited a movie. Choose File > Save to preserve all of your changes.

Tutorial 4: Create a DVD

Now that you've created a movie, it's time to show it off. You'll use the automated DVD features in Adobe Premiere Elements to create and customize an interactive DVD.

1. Set scene markers for the scenes menu.

Open the project that you saved in the previous tutorial. You'll now add DVD scene markers to indicate the start of each scene you want in the scenes menu. In the menu bar, choose DVD > Auto-Generate DVD Markers. In the Auto-Generate DVD Marker dialog box, select At Each Scene, and click OK. This command places a scene marker at the start point for each clip. (Note that a DVD Marker icon appears below the clips in the Sceneline.)

For a movie with many clips, but few scenes, you may prefer to add the markers manually. Just select the first clip of a scene, and choose DVD > Set DVD Marker.

2. Delete extra markers.

Sometimes you don't want a marker at each clip. For example, the second and third clips are really part of the same trolley-riding scene. In the Sceneline, select the clip of the trolley tracks (the third clip), and choose DVD > Clear DVD Marker > DVD Marker At Current Time Indicator.

The three carousel shots should also be together in the same scene. Right-click the second instance of the carousel (the clip showing the words *Pier 39*), and choose Clear DVD Marker. Now, delete the marker on the next clip (with the kids riding the carousel).

3. Choose a DVD template and create menus.

In the task bar, click the Create DVD button ⊙ to switch to the DVD workspace. The Media panel lists the available DVD templates, grouped by theme. Expand the General folder, and then expand the Ocean Waves folder. Drag the Ocean Waves template to the DVD Layout panel. (Notice that DVD templates coordinate with the title templates.)

The main menu appears in the DVD Layout panel. At the bottom of the panel, thumbnails of the main menu and scenes menu appear. (The scenes menu includes buttons for each scene.)

4. Customize the main menu.

Double-click the default title in the main menu. In the Change Text dialog box, type **San Francisco!** and click OK. You can replace the default text for Play Movie and Scene Selection in the same manner. To reposition text, drag it.

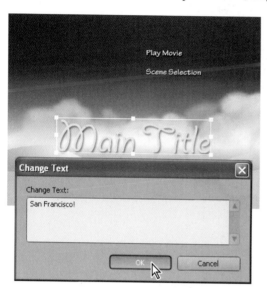

5. Remove title clip from scenes menu.

Click the thumbnail of the scenes menu. The first button shows the clip that contains the movie title, which looks a bit odd. In the Sceneline, right-click the clip that contains the movie title and choose Clear DVD Marker. The scene menu automatically adjusts; now it contains only three scene-selection buttons.

6. Customize scene selection buttons.

Double-click the first scene-selection button. The DVD Marker dialog box appears. The name for scene-selection buttons comes from DVD markers, so if you move, add, or delete scenes, the button names stay current. Click in the Name box, and type **The Ride!**

The first frame of a clip is often not the frame you want displayed for a button. To choose a different frame, drag the pointer over the timecode next to the clip thumbnail until you see the frame you want. Click OK and your custom button will appear on the menu. Rename the second button **Carousel** and the third button **Snapshots**.

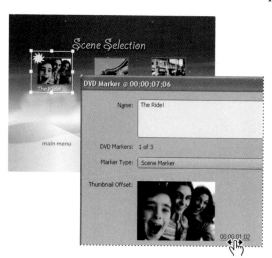

7. Add motion.

Next, you'll create a motion menu, where the clips play within the scene selection buttons. Select the The Ride! button in the DVD Layout panel. In the Properties panel, select Motion Menu Button. Click Apply To All Marker Buttons.

8. Preview the DVD.

To make sure everything works the way you want, preview your DVD before you burn it. In the DVD Layout panel, click Preview DVD. In the Preview DVD panel, click the Play Full Screen button 🖼. Then click the Play button on the DVD menu. When the movie starts, the playback controls become available. Place the pointer over each control to view its name.

When the movie finishes and the main menu appears again, click the Scene Selection button on the DVD menu. Use the arrow keys to navigate, and click the Enter button to start playing the movie from the selected scene. When you're done previewing, click the Exit button, and close the Preview DVD panel. Then save the project.

9. Review settings and burn your DVD.

To prepare video for a DVD, Adobe Premiere Elements compresses it. Compressing video for DVD is time-consuming and can take several hours, depending on the length and complexity of the movie. Although you probably don't want to burn this tutorial project to DVD, you can review the available settings. Click Burn DVD in the DVD Layout panel to view the Burn DVD dialog box. (When finished, click Cancel.)

DVD Settings You can burn directly to a disc if Adobe Premiere Elements supports the media format of your burner. If the format isn't compatible, you can write the DVD to a folder and use the software that came with your DVD burner.

Quality Settings By default, Adobe Premiere Elements fits contents to available space, compressing video only as much as necessary to preserve quality.

Preset Selection The preset selections specify the TV standard for your region so DVD players can play the DVD you create.

Tutorial 5: Capture video into a new project

Now that you know the basics, it's time to create your own movie. The first step: capture your video. Capturing video has never been easier in Adobe Premiere Elements. You connect your camcorder to your computer, start capturing, and Adobe Premiere Elements automatically detects different scenes and adds them directly to your project, ready for editing.

1. Set up your camcorder.

Connect the DV out port of the camcorder to your computer's IEEE 1394 port with an IEEE 1394 cable. (IEEE 1394 is also known by the tradenames FireWire® and i.Link®.) If you have a newer camcorder that supports USB 2.0, you can use a USB 2.0 cable and port. (See the Quick Reference card for more information on connecting your camera.) Turn on the camcorder, and set it to Play/VTR mode.

Adobe Premiere Elements lets you import video, audio, and still images from virtually any device, including camcorders, unprotected DVDs, digital still cameras, MPEG-4 video recorders, and mobile phones. See online Help for more information.

2. Create a project.

Start Adobe Premiere Elements, and then click Capture Video on the welcome screen. In the New Project dialog box, specify a name and location for your project, and click OK. The Capture panel opens.

💡 *To capture video in an existing project, click the Get Media From button* 📸 *in the task bar, and choose Capture.*

If you're capturing from a webcam or HDV camcorder, choose Capture Settings from the More menu. In the Project Settings dialog box, select the appropriate option for Capture Format, and click OK.

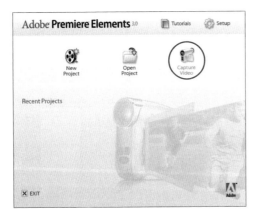

3. Ready, set, capture!

With DV and HDV camcorders, the transport controls at the bottom of the Capture panel let you play, rewind, and fast-forward your video to find the clips you want to capture. You can capture either all your video or specific scenes. (Adobe Premiere Elements detects scenes in your footage, based on when you started and stopped shooting, and creates a clip for each.)

When you're ready to capture, move to the beginning of the first scene, and click Get Video. The status area at the top of the Capture panel indicates whether capturing is in progress and how much space is available on your hard drive.

When you want to stop capturing, click the Stop button. Use the controls to locate and capture any additional scenes. When finished, close the Capture panel, and save your project.

4. Edit your movie

Your clips are in the Sceneline ready for editing. Now combine your creativity with the power of Adobe Premiere Elements to create your first movie!

Chapter 3: Projects and workspaces

Project basics

About projects

Adobe Premiere Elements combines everything you need to create a movie, including video, audio, effects, transitions, and titles into a single file called a *project file*. Adobe Premiere Elements creates a project file for every new project you start. By default, it uses a project preset for the television standard (NTSC or PAL) you selected when you installed the program.

A project file stores only title files and references to the source files that you capture or import, so project files remain fairly small. Because only references to the source files are stored, avoid moving, renaming, or deleting your source files so that Adobe Premiere Elements can continue to locate them.

For more information, see "About workspaces and panels" on page 43.

To start a new blank project

When you start a new project from the welcome screen, you can review the default preset and its settings by clicking the Setup button. You should change the preset only if it doesn't match the specifications of your source media. In that case, you need to create a new preset or install a custom preset if your capture card or video hardware provides one.

Important: Some settings, such as frame rate, size and aspect ratio, can't be changed after a project is created—verify all project settings before starting a project. Using the wrong project settings can adversely affect performance as you work on your project.

1 Do one of the following:

- Start Adobe Premiere Elements, and from the welcome screen, click New Project or Capture Video.

- In Adobe Premiere Elements, choose File > New > Project.

2 In the New Project dialog box, specify a name and location for the project, and click OK.

Note: By default, the folder for a saved project also stores rendered previews, conformed audio files, and captured audio and video. These files are very large, so you should save them to your largest, fastest hard drive. To store these files separately from projects, choose Edit > Preferences > Scratch Disks.

For more information, see "About project settings and presets" on page 41.

To open a project

You can open only one project at a time. (However, you can add media from one project to another.) To ensure that Adobe Premiere Elements can open an existing project, make sure that both the project file (.prel) and the source files used in it are accessible on your computer.

❖ Do one of the following:

• Start Adobe Premiere Elements, and click the project name in the welcome screen. (If the project isn't listed, click Open Project, select the project file, and click Open.)

• In Adobe Premiere Elements, choose File > Open Project, select the project file, and click Open.

• In Windows`, double-click the project file.

Note: Adobe Premiere Elements can open projects made in earlier versions of the program, but earlier versions of Adobe Premiere Elements cannot open projects made in later versions. If you have two or more versions of Adobe Premiere Elements installed, you may need to open a project from within the software rather than by double-clicking the project file.

For more information, see "To locate missing files" on page 40 and "To open a project saved by Auto Save" on page 49.

To locate missing files

Adobe Premiere Elements doesn't store original source files in a project—it references the file name and location of each source file when you import it. If you later move, rename, or delete a source file in Windows, Adobe Premiere Elements opens the Where Is The File dialog box when you next open the project.

In addition to source files, a project also references *preview files*. Preview files allow you to preview effects in real-time without having to render them—a process that can take hours. Preview files can be re-created as often as necessary.

Note: After you create the final movie, you can delete source files if you do not plan to use them in a project again. If you may need to re-edit the movie in the future, archive the project with the Project Archiver before deleting source files.

❖ In the Where Is The File dialog box, choose one of the following options:

Display Only Exact Name Matches Displays only the files that match the name of the missing file when the project was last closed. If you know that the file name has changed, deselect this option.

Select Replaces the missing file with the selected original or replacement file.

Find Starts the Windows XP˙ Search feature.

Skip Previews Skips missing preview files so you aren't asked to find them.

Skip Replaces the missing file with an *offline file*, a blank placeholder for related clips in the Media panel and My Project panel.

Skip All Replaces all missing clips with offline files without asking you for confirmation.

For more information, see "Troubleshooting" in Adobe Premiere Elements Help.

For more information, see "To find an item in a project" on page 77.

Project settings and presets

About project settings and presets

Project settings determine the video and audio format of a project, including video frame rate, aspect ratio, audio sample rate, and bit depth.

When you start a new project, Adobe Premiere Elements applies a project preset to it. A project preset is a collection of preconfigured project settings. In most cases, you can use the default project preset, which is set for 4:3 DV footage for the television standard you specified when you installed Adobe Premiere Elements. NTSC (National Television Standards Committee) is the television standard for the Americas, the Caribbean, Japan, South Korea, and Taiwan; PAL (Phase Alternating Line) is the standard format for Europe, Russia, Africa, the Middle East, India, Australia, New Zealand, the South Pacific, China, and other parts of Asia.

You can't change the project preset after starting a project, so verify the format of your source footage before selecting a project preset. Depending on your source footage, you may need to change the preset or create a new one. If your footage is widescreen, for example, you need to select a Widescreen preset before you start your project; if it's HDV, choose one of the Adobe HDV presets.

If you need to specify lower quality settings for output (such as streaming web video), don't change your project settings—change your export settings instead.

Creating and changing project presets

The default project presets in Adobe Premiere Elements are appropriate for most types of source media, including video from DV camcorders, cameras, DVD discs, and mobile phones. If your source footage requires a custom project preset, you can create one. The procedure for creating a preset differs if you're changing settings for an open project versus establishing settings for a new project. Presets you create can be applied to new projects, and if you want to back up or distribute preset files, you can find them in the Settings subfolder of the Adobe Premiere Elements folder on your hard disk.

If you have a capture card that includes presets for capturing from Adobe Premiere Elements, installing the card's software also installs the presets. Manufacturer-supplied presets are tested with the manufacturer's hardware, so you should not change their settings.

To select a project preset

By default, Adobe Premiere Elements uses a DV preset for the television standard you specify when you install the program. You will need to select a new preset to create new projects in a different format (such as HDV), television standard (such as PAL), or frame aspect ratio (such as widescreen).

1 Start Adobe Premiere Elements

2 In the welcome screen, click Setup ⚙.

3 Select the preset that matches the format and standard of the footage you want to edit. For example, to edit most HDV footage shot on 1080i camcorders in the American market, choose HDV 1080i 30 (Sony 60i).

4 Click Save As Default.

The preset you selected will determine the settings of every new project you create, until you select another preset.

5 In the welcome screen, click New Project .

6 Give the project a name and location. Click OK.

For more information, see "Creating and changing project presets" in Adobe Premiere Elements Help.

To review a project's settings

After you start a project, you can't change most of the project settings, such as frame rate, size, and aspect ratio. However, you can review the settings to make sure that the media you want to add to the project is compatible.

❖ Open the project in Adobe Premiere Elements, and choose Edit > Project Settings > *[category]*.

For more information, see "Settings within a project preset" in Adobe Premiere Elements Help.

Workspaces and panels

About workspaces and panels

A *workspace* is an arrangement of panels optimized for a particular task. Adobe Premiere Elements has two preconfigured workspaces: one for editing video, the other for authoring DVDs. You can modify these to meet your specific needs. Adobe Premiere Elements will retain your modifications until you further modify them, or restore them to their original configurations.

Adobe Premiere Elements comes with workspaces optimized for the two major phases of a project: editing a movie, and authoring a DVD. You can easily change from one workspace to the other, depending on the tasks you need to accomplish.

You perform tasks primarily in panels. Each workspace contains a default set of docked panels useful for the tasks typical of the respective phase. The following three panels are common to both workspaces in Adobe Premiere Elements.

Media Lets you import or capture media, and select media, templates, and effects for use in your movie. There are five different views of the Media panel. Four of these are visible in the Edit workspace; three are visible in the DVD workspace. Each view opens when its respective button, on the left of the Media panel, is clicked.

• **Available Media** 🎞 Lets you view, sort, and select media from all that you have captured or imported into your project. The Available Media view itself has two views, selectable by buttons at the lower left of the Media panel: List view ▤ , and Icon view ▦ .

• **Get Media From** 📇 Shows buttons for five types of sources from which you can acquire media for your movie. Clicking one of these buttons will open the correct application for importing or capturing from the respective type of source.

• **Effects And Transitions** 🎨 Shows groups of effects, transitions, and presets you can use in your movie. You can search for any of these by typing its name into the search field toward the top of the panel, or browse for it by clicking the triangle to the left of any group heading.

• **Title Templates** 🗏 Shows groups of preformatted titles you can use in your movie. You can browse for a template by clicking the triangle to the left of any group heading.

• **DVD Templates** 🗐 Shows groups of preformatted DVD templates you can use as guides for creating DVD menus. You can browse for these by clicking the triangle to the left of any group heading. This view is visible only in the DVD workspace.

Properties Lets you view and adjust properties of a clip selected in the Monitor, DVD Layout, or My Project panels.

My Project Lets you assemble your media into the desired order and edit clips. You can preview the clips in the My Project panel in the Monitor panel.

The My Project panel has two views: the Sceneline, which allows you quickly to arrange your media, adding titles, transitions and effects; and the Timeline which helps you trim, layer, and synchronize your media.

Adobe Premiere Elements also provides specialized panels for tasks such as capturing video, previewing clips and movies, and laying out DVD menus.

Default Edit workspace
A. *Monitor panel* **B.** *Task bar* **C.** *Media panel* **D.** *Sceneline view of the My Project panel* **E.** *Properties panel*

For more information, see "To choose a workspace" on page 45 and "About the Available Media view of the Media panel" on page 75.

To choose a workspace

Depending on the workspace you choose, certain key panels become available. For example, the Monitor panel is available in the Edit workspace. In either workspace, you can rearrange panels to better suit your working style. Your customized arrangement appears whenever you access a workspace.

❖ Do one of the following:

• In the task bar, click a workspace button, Edit Movie 🖳 or Create DVD 💿.

• Choose Window > Workspace, and then choose a workspace.

For more information, see "Customizing workspaces" in Adobe Premiere Elements Help.

To open panel menus

Most panels include menus that appear when you click the More button. In addition, all panels have context menus, the content of which depends on the current task or mode. The commands in the menus are specific to individual panels.

- To open panel menus, click the More button in the panel.
- To open panel context menus, right-click in the panel.

Info panel

The Info panel displays information about a selected item in the Available Media view of the Media panel or the My Project panel. For clips, the Info panel displays information such as duration, In point, Out point, and the location of the cursor. The information displayed may vary depending on factors such as the media type and the current panel. For example, the Info panel displays different sets of information for an empty space in the Timeline, a rectangle in the Title panel, and a clip in the Media panel.

In the Info panel, the Video entry indicates the frame rate, frame size, dimensions, and pixel aspect ratio; the Audio entry indicates the sample rate, bit depth, and channels.

How To panel

The How To panel provides a group of how-to's for each stage of a project. How-to's include a short set of instructions that help you quickly complete common video-editing and DVD authoring tasks. When you click task bar buttons to change the workspace, the How To panel automatically displays related how-to's. You can also navigate between groups of related how-to's by using the pop-up menu in the panel. To return to the list of how-to's for the current workspace, click the Home button 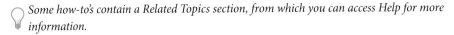.

Some how-to's contain a Related Topics section, from which you can access Help for more information.

To open the How To panel

❖ Click the How To button .

Undoing and saving changes

Undoing changes incrementally

If you change your mind about an edit or effect, Adobe Premiere Elements provides several ways to undo your work. You can undo only those actions that alter video content; for example, you can undo an edit, but you cannot undo scrolling a panel.

- To undo or redo the most recent change, choose Edit > Undo. (You can sequentially undo a series of recent changes.)

- To undo a change, and all successive changes, that occurred since you last opened a project, delete it from the History panel.

- To stop a change that Adobe Premiere Elements is processing (for example, when you see a progress bar), press Esc.

- To undo all changes made since you last saved the project, choose File > Revert.

To undo changes made before you last saved a project, try opening a previous version in the Premiere Auto-Save folder. Then choose File > Save As to store the project outside of the Premiere Auto-Save folder. The number of changes you can undo depends on the Auto Save preference settings.

For more information, see "To back up a project with Auto Save" on page 49.

To undo any previous change

The History panel records the changes you make to a project. For example, each time you add a clip, insert a marker, or apply an effect, the History panel adds that action to the bottom of its list. The tool or command you used appears in the panel along with an identifying icon. You can use the panel to quickly undo several changes. When you select a change in the panel, the project returns to the state of the project at the time of that change. The more recent changes turn gray and disappear when you make your next change.

The History panel records changes only for the current session. Closing a project or choosing the Revert command clears the History panel. While the panel lists most changes, it does not list individual changes within some panels, nor does it list program-wide changes, such as Preferences settings.

Note: The History panel is hidden by default to conserve screen space. To display the History panel, choose Window > History.

- To display the History panel, choose Window > History.

- To select a change in the History panel, click it.

- To delete a selected change, choose Delete from the More menu in the History panel, and then click OK. Or, click the Delete icon 🗑, and then click OK.

- To move around in the History panel, drag the slider or the scroll bar in the panel. Or, click the More button, and choose Step Forward or Step Backward.

- To clear all changes from the History panel, click the More button and choose Clear History, and then click OK.

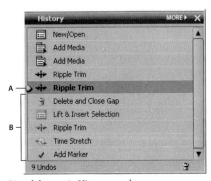

List of changes in History panel
A. Selected change B. Later changes that will be replaced by next change

For more information, see "Undoing changes incrementally" on page 47.

To save a project

Saving a project saves your editing decisions, references to source files, and the most recent arrangement of panels. Protect your work by saving often.

- To save the currently open project, choose File > Save.

- To save a copy of a project and continue working in the new copy, choose File > Save As, specify a location and file name, and click Save.

- To save a copy of a project and continue working in the original project, choose File > Save A Copy, specify a location and file name, and click Save.

To specify where Adobe Premiere Elements stores project-related files, such as captured video and audio, and video and audio previews, see "To set up a scratch disk" in Adobe Premiere Elements Help.

For more information, see "To back up a project with Auto Save" on page 49.

To back up a project with Auto Save

To more easily revisit editing decisions or recover from a crash, enable the Auto Save option. This option automatically saves backup project files to the Adobe Premiere Elements Auto-Save folder at a specified time interval. For example, you can set Adobe Premiere Elements to save a backup copy every 15 minutes, producing a series of files that represent the state of your project at each interval.

Automatic saving serves as an alternative to the Undo command, depending on how much the project changes between each save. Because project files are quite small compared to source video files, archiving many versions of a project consumes relatively little disk space.

1 Choose Edit > Preferences > Auto Save.

2 Do any of the following, and then click OK:

• Select Automatically Save Projects, and type the number of minutes after which Adobe Premiere Elements will save the project.

• Type a number for the Maximum Project Versions to specify how many versions of each project file you want to save. For example, if you type 5, Adobe Premiere Elements saves five versions of each project you open.

Note: *Each time you open a project, you must save it at least once before the Auto Save option takes effect.*

For more information, see "To save a project" on page 48.

To open a project saved by Auto Save

1 Do either of the following:

• Start Adobe Premiere Elements, and click Open Project.

• In Adobe Premiere Elements, choose File > Open Project.

2 In the project folder, open the file in the Adobe Premiere Elements Auto-Save folder. (If no files are available, the Auto Save preference may be turned off.)

Note: *The first time you start Adobe Premiere Elements after a crash, it returns a prompt asking if you want to open the last version of your project saved by Auto Save.*

For more information, see "To open a project" on page 40.

Chapter 4: Adding media

Adding media basics

Methods for adding media

There are three basic methods for adding media to your projects: *capturing* from tape or live sources, *importing* files from other types of storage, or *recording* from a microphone. Capturing typically involves recording video and audio directly to a hard drive from either a videotape playing in real time or a live audio or video source. Importing typically involves copying video, audio, or still images to a hard drive location from memory cards, thumb drives, DVDs, CDs, or other hard drive locations. Recording is used only for recording narrations.

Whether you add media to your project by importing, capturing or recording, each file will be represented by its own thumbnail in the Available Media view of the Media panel. Each of these representations is called a *clip*. Clips, whether they contain audio, video, or still images, are the building blocks of your movies.

Common sources of media files

Adobe Premiere Elements lets you add video, audio, graphics, and still images to your project from numerous sources. In the Get Media From view of the Media panel, various buttons let you access the following items:

- Camcorders
- Digital cameras
- Webcams
- Computer microphones
- Videotapes and audiotapes (analog and digital)
- DVDs and CDs
- Memory cards, such as CompactFlash (CF), Secure Digital (SD), and Memory Stick (MS)
- Mobile phones
- Audio, video, and still-image files already in folders on your computer

Setting up for capturing

Preparing a project for video capture

Before you capture digital video, you need to create a project with a preset that matches the footage you will be capturing. For best results, make sure that the preset you choose matches the format (DV or HDV), television standard (NTSC or PAL), and frame aspect ratio (Standard or Widescreen) used when you shot your footage.

If the video you are capturing was shot in widescreen (16:9) format, be sure to choose a widescreen preset.

If the video you are capturing was shot with an HDV camcorder, choose one of the following presets:

- HDV 1080i 25 (Sony 50i)

- HDV 1080i 30 (Sony 60i)

- HDV 720p 30

For more information, see "To start a new blank project" on page 39 and "To select a project preset" on page 42.

System requirements for capturing

Adobe Premiere Elements includes all the necessary tools to transfer the footage from your camcorder so that you can begin assembling your movie. You simply connect your camcorder to your computer and then use the Adobe Premiere Elements Capture command.

Note: *You can also get video, audio, and still-image files from certain digital still-image cameras, mobile phones supporting Nokia PC Suite 6.0 and later, DVD camcorders, and other removable media using the Media Downloader feature. Not all video devices and file types are supported. (See "To add files from DVDs, still cameras, mobile phones, tapeless camcorders, and other devices" on page 72 and "File types you can import" on page 66.)*

Before you capture video, make sure that your system is set up appropriately for working with digital video. Consider the following general guidelines for ensuring that you have a DV-capable system.

Ports for connecting to the video device Your computer must have an IEEE 1394 port (also known as FireWire or i.Link) or a USB 2.0 port with a USB Video Class 1.0 driver installed. These ports might be built into your computer or available on a PCI or PC card that you install yourself. A number of computers include onboard IEEE 1394 and USB 2.0 cards. To capture from a camcorder through the USB 2.0 port, your camcorder must support USB Video Class 1.0, a standard that defines the minimum capabilities for streaming DV video using the USB 2.0 port.

Hard disk speed The speed at which data is transmitted, called the *data transfer rate* (often shortened to *data rate*), in DV format is 3.6 MB per second. The data transfer rate of your hard disk should meet or exceed this rate if it is to capture DV. To achieve this rate, your hard disk must be able to operate at 7200 rpm. Most hard disks manufactured in the last five years have this capability. To confirm the rate or rpm speed of your hard disk, see your computer or hard disk documentation.

Hard disk space Five minutes of DV-AVI video occupies about 1 GB of hard disk space. Allow enough space, not only for the source footage you will capture, but also for the preview files and final rendered movie and DVD folders, should you choose to make these.

Note: Make certain before capturing that you have enough hard disk space for the length of footage you will capture. Before capture, the Capture panel shows the amount of free disk space remaining. During capture, it shows the duration of footage that can be captured using the remaining free space.

Defragmenting hard disks Periodically defragment your hard disk. Writing to a fragmented disk can cause disruptions in your hard disk's write speed, causing you to lose, or drop, frames as you capture. You can use the defragmentation utility included with Windows XP', located in Start > All Programs (or Programs if you are using the Classic Mode display) > Accessories > System Tools > Disk Defragmenter.

For more information, see "Connecting to a digital camcorder" on page 55 and "Methods for adding media" on page 51.

Devices you can capture from

Adobe Premiere Elements allows you to capture video, audio, or both from several types of devices:

- Those that have IEEE 1394 or USB 2.0 ports, provided your computer also has one of these. Most camcorders and tape decks in the DV and HDV formats, and most webcams, have one of these ports. You can also capture video or still images from webcams with USB 1.0 ports.

Ports and plugs for capture of digital audio, video, and stills
A. *IEEE 1394* ***B.*** *USB*

Note: *Most camcorders with USB ports use them for transferring still images only, not video. Check your camcorder user guide to see whether it supports video capture through USB 2.0.*

- Those that have analog audio-video output plugs, provided your computer has analog audio-video inputs. You can also capture from these devices if your computer has IEEE 1394 or USB 2.0 ports, provided you have a digital camcorder or analog-to-digital (AV DV) converter that can convert analog signals to digital and output to one of these ports on your computer.

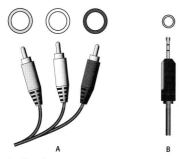

Analog plugs
A. *RCA analog video and audio plugs for video (yellow), left audio (white), and right audio (red).* **B.** *Stereo mini-plug, typically used with stereo audio devices*

Device control allows you conveniently to control your source camcorder or tape deck from the Capture panel. You can use device control with tape-based devices of either of these types:

- Those that have IEEE 1394 or USB 2.0 ports, provided your computer also has one of these. Most camcorders and tape decks in the DV and HDV formats have one of these ports.

- Those that have LANC, control-L, control-M, or RS 422 control plugs, provided you have a serial controller for your computer that also makes use of the control protocol used by your device.

You can capture from devices lacking these ports and plugs, but you will not be able to use device control with them.

For more information, see "To set up for narration" on page 179.

Connecting to a digital camcorder

Adobe Premiere Elements supports a wide range of digital camcorders, making it easy to capture video source files. To capture digital video, connect your DV or HDV camcorder to your computer's IEEE 1394 port or USB 2.0 port. If your computer does not have a built-in IEEE 1394 or USB 2.0 port, you can purchase port cards (see your computer's documentation for more information). If your camcorder does not include the appropriate cable, you can purchase one at a computer, camera, or consumer electronics store.

Some camcorders require that you use the power adapter to activate the IEEE 1394 port. Other camcorders may go into sleep or other inactive mode if left in camera mode without being activated for a period of time, even if connected to a power adapter.

Note: You cannot capture HDV video through USB ports.

For more information, see "To add files from DVDs, still cameras, mobile phones, tapeless camcorders, and other devices" on page 72.

Connecting to a camcorder using USB 2.0

Only the newest models of DV camcorders support video capture through USB 2.0 ports. Many camcorders hold USB ports for downloading still-image files only. If your camcorder has both an IEEE 1394 port and a USB port, use the IEEE 1394 port for video capture. Also, you cannot capture HDV video through USB 2.0 ports. For the latest information about support of USB 2.0 camcorders by Adobe Premiere Elements, see the Adobe website.

 For more information, see "Connecting to an analog device" in Adobe Premiere Elements Help.

Capturing video

Capture panel overview

Use the Capture panel to monitor the video and access all of the capture commands. This panel includes a video preview area, recording controls, a disk-space indicator, and a timecode display. From the Capture panel menu, accessed when you click the More button, you can view and edit your current capture settings. You open the Capture panel by clicking the Get Media From button 🎥 in the task bar and selecting Capture. You can also open it by clicking the Capture Video button on the welcome screen, which appears when the application launches.

Capture panel
A. Status area B. Preview area C. Capture menu D. Device controls

Note: *For details about troubleshooting capture problems, see the "Troubleshooting" section in Help.*

Capturing with device control

If the source of your footage is a tape-based device, such as a camcorder or tape deck, with an IEEE 1394 or USB 2.0 port, or if you use a serial device controller with an analog device, you can capture your footage using only the controls in the Capture panel. *Device control* is a convenient way to locate and capture scenes. It allows you to use the Capture panel controls (Play, Fast Forward, Rewind, Pause, Stop, and Record) to control your device.

The device control settings are located in the Preferences dialog box (choose Edit > Preferences > Device Control, or, in the Capture panel, click the More button and choose Device Control). The Device Control section is also where you specify either IEEE 1394 capture (DV/HDV Device Control) or USB 2.0 capture (USB Video Class 1.0 - Device Control).

Capture panel controls
A. Previous Scene B. Next Scene C. Rewind D. Step Back E. Play F. Shuttle G. Step Forward H. Fast Forward I. Stop

> *If you are capturing only a portion of a tape, as opposed to capturing an entire tape, capture at least three seconds of additional footage (called handles) at both the beginning and end of the capture to ensure a margin of error during capture. Handles also allow for cleaner transitions and more flexibility when you trim your clips.*

For more information, see "Capturing without device control" on page 60 and "To activate or deactivate Scene Detect" on page 60.

To capture from DV and HDV camcorders

1 Connect the DV or HDV camcorder to your computer by using an IEEE 1394 connection or, for some DV camcorders, a USB 2.0 port. The IEEE 1394 port on your camcorder may be marked DV IN/OUT, i.Link, or IEEE 1394. The USB 2.0 port is marked by the USB icon ⟷ .

Note: *Don't connect the camcorder to both the IEEE 1394 and USB 2.0 ports at the same time.*

2 Turn the camcorder on and set it to playback mode, which might be labeled either VTR, VCR, or Play. Avoid setting the camcorder to a recording mode, such as Camera or Movie.

3 Start Adobe Premiere Elements.

4 If this is your first time capturing from a given device, or if you have changed devices since last capturing with Adobe Premiere Elements, click Setup on the welcome screen.

5 In the Setup dialog box, select the preset that matches the format and television standard of your device. For example, if you are capturing from an HDV camcorder, choose the appropriate HDV preset. Click Save As Default.

6 From the welcome screen, select New Project or Open Project.

7 Choose Edit > Preferences > Device Control, and do one of the following:

• If you want to capture video through an IEEE 1394 cable, select DV/HDV Device Control from the Devices pop-up menu. Click OK.

• If you want to capture video through a USB 2.0 port, select USB Video Class 1.0 - Device Control from the Devices pop-up menu. Click OK.

8 Click the Get Media From button ▓ in the task bar, and choose Capture.

9 In the Capture panel, click the More button and select or deselect Scene Detect and Capture To Timeline. Capturing to the Timeline automatically assembles all captured clips in the My Project panel, in the order in which they are captured, providing a quick way to prepare your movie for editing.

10 Click the More button again; then select Capture Settings.

11 If it isn't already selected, select the format of your video source from the Capture Format pop-up menu: DV Capture, HDV Capture, or WDM Capture.

12 Use the Capture panel controls or the Current Position Timecode display to locate the scene you want to capture.

• To use the Current Position Timecode, drag the display or click it and enter the timecode you want.

• To use Scene Detect, advance to the next or previous scenes by clicking the Next Scene button ▓ or the Previous Scene button ▓ .

Note: Activating any application window other than the Capture panel stops the capture. If you want the capture to continue without interruption, do not access any other panel.

13 Click Get Video.

If you are capturing DV footage, you will see a preview of your video in the Capture panel. If you are capturing HDV footage, only the word Capturing will appear there, and you will able to view the playback on the HDV device itself.

14 To stop the capture before the tape reaches its end, click Stop Capture.

15 Do one of the following:

• If you chose Scene Detect, you can also use the Next Scene and Previous Scene buttons to move to the respective scene.

• If you didn't choose Scene Detect and you captured only a segment of your video, you can repeat this procedure to locate and capture another segment of video.

16 When you finish capturing, close the Capture panel.

To operate some Capture panel controls with the keyboard, see the shortcuts in the tool tip for each control button. (Hold your pointer over a button to see its tool tip.)

For more information, see "To activate or deactivate Scene Detect" on page 60 and "To activate or deactivate Capture To Timeline" on page 61.

Capturing without device control

If the device holding your source footage does not have an IEEE 1394 or USB 2.0 port, and if you do not use a serial device controller to control an analog device, you cannot use device control to control your device's transport mechanism with the controls in the Capture panel. You can nevertheless capture video and audio from this device by controlling it manually. For example, you can capture video from an analog camcorder if you have analog audio and video input jacks on your computer, or if you use a digital camcorder or AV DV converter to convert the analog signal into a digital form your computer can use.

For more information see "To capture from camcorders, tape decks, or standard Windows devices without device control" in Adobe Premiere Elements Help.

To activate or deactivate Scene Detect

By default, Adobe Premiere Elements uses scene detection when capturing clips. Scene Detect analyzes video for scene breaks indicated by the tape's time/date stamp. DV and HDV camcorders add a time/date stamp to the tape each time you press Record. With Scene Detect active, Adobe Premiere Elements captures a separate clip at each scene break it detects, and then places each clip into the Available Media view of the Media panel. Although it is usually most efficient to have a separate clip for each scene, you can deactivate Scene Detect if you want to capture an entire tape without breaking it into separate clips.

❖ In the Capture panel, click the More button and select Scene Detect. A check mark indicates that the feature is activated.

To activate or deactivate Capture To Timeline

By default, when Adobe Premiere Elements completes a capture, it places the captured clips into the My Project panel in the order they were captured. This feature is especially convenient because it creates a timeline that duplicates the order of the clips on your tape and makes it easier to locate and delete unwanted clips. This feature is also useful if you record scenes in roughly the order you want them to remain.

You can deactivate this feature if you plan to place clips in an order different from that of the original tape.

❖ In the Capture panel, click the More button and select Capture To Timeline. A check mark indicates that the feature is activated. All captured clips will also reside in the Available Media view of the Media panel.

Capturing stop-motion video

Using stop-motion video, you can make inanimate objects appear to move, or show a flower grow and bloom in seconds. In this mode, you capture single video frames at widely spaced time intervals for later playback at faster frame rates.

You create stop-motion animations or time-lapse videos using the Stop Motion button in the Capture panel. You can capture frames either from prerecorded tape or from a live camera feed. You manually capture stop-motion frames, or automatically capture frames at set intervals in Time Lapse mode.

Note: You cannot capture stop-motion video from an HDV source.

To set up for stop-motion or time-lapse capture

1 Connect your device to your computer and turn it on.

Note: If it is a WDM device, you may need to turn it on by double-clicking its icon in the Windows My Computer folder. Doing so may open a Windows video preview window. Close this before proceeding.

2 If it is a tape-based device, do one of the following:

• If capturing live from a camcorder, place the camcorder in Camera mode.

• If capturing from videotape, place the device in Play, VTR, or VCR mode.

3 Click the Get Media From button 🎞 in the Media panel.

4 Click the DV Camcorder, HDV Camcorder, Webcam button 📷 in the Media panel.

Adobe Premiere Elements opens the Capture panel, and opens the Available Media view of the Media panel.

5 Click the More button and select or deselect Capture To Timeline.

Capture To Timeline will drop each frame into the My Project panel as it is captured.

6 Click the More button again; then select Capture Settings.

7 If it isn't already selected, select the format of your video source from the Capture Format pop-up menu:

• If you are capturing from a DV camcorder or are converting an analog signal through an AV DV converter or digital camcorder, select DV Capture.

• If your source is a webcam or other WDM device, select WDM Capture.

8 Click the More button again, and select Device Control.

9 Select Stop Motion Capture.

This will open the Stop Motion Capture preferences in the Preferences dialog box.

10 Set the Onion Skinning and Playback options. Onion Skinning allows you to see frames previously captured superimposed on your video source. This helps you position figures you want to animate.

Opacity Level Sets the level of opacity for the Onion Skins. Raise this number to make the onion skins less transparent.

Number of Skins Sets the number of onion skins visible at one time.

Frame Rate Sets the number of frames per second.

To capture stop-motion from a live video source

1 Click the Get Media From button in the Media panel.

2 Click the DV Camcorder, HDV Camcorder, Webcam button in the Media panel.

Adobe Premiere Elements opens the Capture panel, and opens the Available Media view of the Media panel.

3 Click the Stop Motion button in the Capture panel.

4 Click the Create New Stop Motion button in the middle of the Capture panel preview pane.

The Capture panel shows a preview of your live video source.

5 To see onion skins—overlays of previous frames captured—select the Onion Skinning option in the lower right of the Capture panel. You can use this to line up figures you animate.

6 Point the camera at a subject and click Grab Frame whenever the Capture panel displays a frame that you want to save to the hard disk. Each frame you grab will appear as a BMP file in Available Media with a sequential number in its filename.

7 Click the Close button ⊠ in the upper right of the Capture panel.

A dialog box will ask whether to save the captured images as a movie file.

8 Do one of the following:

- To save the captured images as a single movie file, as well as a set of still images, click Yes. Then, give the new movie a name and location, and click Save.

- To save the captured images only as individual still photos, click No.

Depending on your choice, Adobe Premiere Elements will place the still images, or the still images and movie file, in Available Media. Additionally, if you had Capture to Timeline selected, Adobe Premiere Elements will place the still images, but not the movie file, into the My Project panel.

To capture in Time Lapse mode

Use Time Lapse mode to let your computer grab frames at intervals you determine. You can thus reduce a lengthy event, such as a sunset or a flower blooming, to a very short span. Time Lapse can be used with videotape or live camera sources.

1 Click the Get Media From button 🎥 in the Media panel.

2 Click the DV Camcorder, HDV Camcorder, Webcam button 📷 in the Media panel.

Adobe Premiere Elements opens the Capture panel and the Available Media view of the Media panel.

3 Click the Stop Motion button 🎥 in the Capture panel.

4 Click the Create New Stop Motion button in the middle of the Capture panel preview pane.

The Capture panel shows a preview of your live video source.

5 To see onion skins—overlays of previous frames captured—select the Onion Skinning option in the lower right of the Capture panel. You can use this to line up figures you animate.

6 Select Time Lapse in the lower left of the Capture panel.

7 Click Set Time ⊕.

8 Under Frequency, drag any of the time controls (Hrs, Min, Sec) to set the interval at which you want the computer to grab frames. For example, setting Frequency to 1 minute will make the computer capture one frame every minute.

9 Under Duration, drag any of the time controls to set the length of the capture session. For example, a duration of 5 hours will make the computer capture frames, at the frequency you set, for a duration of 5 hours, then stop.

10 Click OK.

11 Click the Start Time Lapse button.

Adobe Premiere Elements will begin capturing frames at the rate you specified. Toward the upper left of the Capture panel, Next Frame indicates the time of the next scheduled frame grab.

12 When the time-lapse capture is done, click the Close button ✕ in the upper right of the Capture panel.

A dialog box will ask whether to save the captured images as a movie file.

13 Do one of the following:

- To save the captured images as a single movie file, as well as a set of still images, click Yes. Then, give the new movie a name and location, and click Save.

- To save the captured images only as individual still photos, click No.

Depending on your choice, Adobe Premiere Elements will place the still images, or the still images and movie file, in Available Media. Additionally, if you had Capture to Timeline selected, Adobe Premiere Elements will place the still images, but not the movie file, into the My Project panel.

To delete the previous stop-motion or time-lapse frame

While grabbing stop-motion frames, you may occasionally want to delete the last frame you grabbed, for example, after unintentionally capturing an intrusive hand or object.

❖ Click the Delete Frame button 🗑 at the lower left of the Capture panel.

Adobe Premiere Elements will delete the last frame you captured.

Note: You can delete additional frames, starting with the last one shot and working backwards, by clicking the Delete Frame button repeatedly.

To preview a stop-motion or time-lapse movie

You can preview a stop-motion or time-lapse movie at any time while building one. For example, you may want to see whether you are getting the expected results or whether to delete some frames before proceeding.

1 With the Capture panel in Stop Motion mode, select the Preview option in the lower right of the Capture panel.

2 In the Capture panel, click the Play button 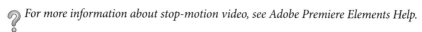.

The Capture panel will show a preview of the movie made from the stop-motion frames you have grabbed so far.

3 Deselect the Preview option to return to grabbing frames.

For more information about stop-motion video, see Adobe Premiere Elements Help.

About timecode

Timecode numbers represent the location of a frame in a video clip. Many camcorders record timecode as part of the video signal. The timecode format is based on the number of frames per second (fps) that the camcorder records and the number of frames per second that the video displays upon playback. Video has a standard frame rate that is either 29.97 fps for NTSC video (the North American and Japanese TV standard) or 25 fps for PAL video (the European TV standard). Timecode describes a frame's location in the format of hours;minutes;seconds;frames. For example, 01;20;15;10 specifies that the displayed frame is located 1 hour, 20 minutes, 15 seconds, and 10 frames into the scene.

Adding files to a project

File types you can import

Your choice of footage to include in your movie is not limited to the clips that you capture. You can use other image, video, and audio files that reside on your computer. You only need to add them to your Adobe Premiere Elements project to begin working with them. In some cases, added files can retain a link to the Adobe application in which they were created. This allows you to open the file's original application from within Adobe Premiere Elements, make changes, and immediately see the results in Adobe Premiere Elements.

Except where noted, you can import the following file types using the Get Media From button 🗃 in the task bar. Added files are visible in the Available Media view of the Media panel.

Video file types
- AVI Movie (.avi)
- Flash˙ (.swf)
- Filmstrip (.flm)
- MPEG Movie (.mpeg, .vob, .mod, .mpe, .mpg, .m2v, .mp2, .mpv, .m2p, .m2t)
- Windows Media (.wmv, .asf)
- QuickTime Movie (.mov, .3gp, .3g2, .mp4, .m4a, .m4v)

Note: To import video from mobile phones (.3gp and .mp4) you must have QuickTime 6.5.2 or later installed on your computer.

Audio file types
- Dolby˙ AC-3 (.ac3)
- Macintosh˙ Audio AIFF (.aif, .aiff)
- mp3˙ Audio (.mp3)
- MPEG˙ Audio (.mpeg, .mpg, .mpa, .mpe, .m2a)
- QuickTime (.mov, .m4a)
- Windows Media (.wma)
- Windows WAVE (.wav)

Note: Dolby AC-3 is imported as a stand-alone .ac3 file or as part of an encoded audio file in a .vob (DVD) or .mod (JVC Everio) file, but exported as Dolby Digital Stereo only.

Still-image file types

- Adobe Illustrator Art (.ai)

- Adobe Premiere Elements title (.prtl)

- Bitmap (.bmp, .dib, .rle)

- Compuserve GIF (.gif)

- Encapsulated PostScript (.eps)

- Icon (.ico)

- JPEG, JPEG 2000 (.jpg, .jpe, .jpeg, .jfif, jp2)

- Macintosh PICT (.pct, .pic, .pict)

- PCX (.pcx)

- Photoshop (.psd)

- Portable Network Graphic (.png)

- RAW (.raw, .raf, .crw, .cr2, .mrw, .nef, .orf, .dng, .ptx)

- TIFF (.tif, .tiff, LZW compression)

- Truevision Targa (.tga, .icb, .vst, .vda)

For more information, see "File types available for export" on page 215 and "To locate missing files" on page 40.

Adding video files

You can add a single file, multiple files, or an entire folder of files. Before you add video files that you did not capture yourself, make sure that you can view the video outside of Adobe Premiere Elements. Usually, double-clicking a video file opens a playback application, such as Windows Media Player. (Be sure to use the most up-to-date version of Windows Media Player.) If you can play back your file in the player application, you're usually able to use that file in Adobe Premiere Elements.

Note: To play back VOB files, use the DVD player that came with your DVD burner.

When adding video files, consider the following:

MPEG files An MPEG file that plays in Windows Media Player might not be able to be imported or played in Adobe Premiere Elements, because either the file is in a format that Adobe Premiere Elements doesn't support, or the compressor used to create the file isn't compatible with the Adobe Premiere Elements decompressor. Many of these problematic MPEG files are downloaded from the Internet. Windows Media Player can usually play these MPEG files because the compatibility requirements for playing compressed files are less stringent than the requirements for editing them.

Note: The first time you import an MPEG2 file, you may be asked to activate the MPEG2 component. The instructions for doing this will appear in the Component Activation dialog box. Component activation comes free of charge.

Frame sizes You can add video and sequence files with frame sizes up to 4096 x 4096 pixels.

EPS files You can scale EPS files in Adobe Premiere Elements to any size without them becoming jagged or pixelated.

Type 1 AVI clips These files must be rendered before you can preview them from your DV camcorder. To render a Type 1 AVI clip, add it to the Timeline view of the My Project panel and build a preview file of that section of the Timeline by pressing Enter. You know if the clip needs to be rendered by the red line above the clip in the Timeline.

DVD files If you want to add video from a non-commercial DVD, such as one that you burned, or from a DVD camcorder, use the Media Downloader and select the VOB files you want. If the DVD is a motion-picture disc that uses copy protection, you cannot add the files.

For more information, see "Processing interlaced video fields," "To activate a component," and "To specify field processing options for a clip" in Adobe Premiere Elements Help.

For more information, see "To add files from a hard drive" on page 72 and "To add files from DVDs, still cameras, mobile phones, tapeless camcorders, and other devices" on page 72.

Adding audio files

When adding audio files, consider the following:

Stereo and mono files You can add many of the stereo audio files that you can open in another audio player, such as Windows Media Player, to Adobe Premiere Elements. To create a stereo version of a mono file, Adobe Premiere Elements copies the mono channel to both the left and right channel in the new stereo track. In this case, both channels contain the same information.

5.1 surround sound files Importing clips containing 5.1 audio adds a 5.1-channel audio track to Adobe Premiere Elements.

mp3 and WMA files Formats such as mp3 and WMA are compressed using a method that reduces some of the original audio quality. To play back compressed audio, Adobe Premiere Elements (like most video editing applications) must decompress and possibly alter the file's sample rate. Compressing can degrade the audio quality.

CD files If you want to add audio from a CD, you must first copy, or *rip,* the audio tracks to your hard drive using another application. Windows Media Player, included with Windows XP, can perform this task. You can also use Adobe Audition to rip the CD at various quality settings and perform complex audio-processing functions on the file. If you plan to publicly air or distribute your movie, make sure that you own the copyright or have licensed the copyright to any CD audio you use.

Internet files If you download music from the Internet for use in your projects, be aware that some files, notably WMA (Windows Media Audio) and AAC (QuickTime) files may have pre-encoded settings that don't allow you to play the file back in Adobe Premiere Elements.

 For more information, see "About conformed audio files" in Adobe Premiere Elements Help.

Adding still images

By default, Adobe Premiere Elements scales still images to fit the project frame size. This means that if you created an image that is larger than your project frame size, when you add it to your project, Adobe Premiere Elements will reduce its size so that it fits within the frame of your project. You can override this behavior and instead have Adobe Premiere Elements add your files at the size at which they were created. You can also set the default duration for all still images that you add. (See "To change the default duration for still images" on page 71.)

You can also add animations, which usually are saved as a sequence of numbered still-image files. (See "Adding an animation or still-image sequence" in Adobe Premiere Elements Help.

When adding still-image files, consider the following:

Adobe Photoshop and Adobe Photoshop Elements files Adobe Premiere Elements works well with images and video templates you create in Photoshop Elements or Photoshop CS and later. You can create Photoshop still images by using the File > New > Photoshop File command in Adobe Premiere Elements, and subsequently edit images that you can use in your movie projects. For example, to create a still image with the correct frame size and pixel aspect ratio for your current project, choose File > New > Photoshop File. (See "Creating Photoshop files in Adobe Premiere Elements" on page 243.)

Or you can create a video graphic using the File > New > Blank File command in Photoshop Elements or the File > New command in Photoshop CS as a starting point, and then using one of the DV or HDV document presets. These presets are optimized for video output. (See Photoshop Help for more information.)

Note: If you use another application to create your still images, search for "square-pixel footage" in Adobe Premiere Elements Help for information on ideal frame sizes.

JPEG files If you are having trouble importing JPEG files to Adobe Premiere Elements, open them in Photoshop Elements and resave them. Then try to import them again to Adobe Premiere Elements.

TIFF images You can add files from Photoshop 3.0 or later. However, Adobe Premiere Elements doesn't support 16-bit TIFF images created in Photoshop or other applications. Empty (transparent) areas of nonflattened Photoshop files appear transparent in Adobe Premiere Elements because the transparency is stored as an alpha channel.

RGB mode When you are editing or creating your still images, make sure that you do all of your work in RGB mode. For more information, consult your product's user guide about color management. RGB mode produces colors that are suitable for video.

Frame sizes You can add still images with frame sizes up to 4096 x 4096 pixels. For best results, create files with a frame size at least as large as the frame size of your video so that you don't have to enlarge, or scale up, the image in Adobe Premiere Elements. When you scale up an image, it often becomes pixelated. If you plan to scale up an image, prepare it at a larger frame size than the project. For example, if you plan to scale up an image 200%, prepare the image at double the project frame size before you add it. To determine the frame size of your video, right-click it in the Available Media view of the Media panel or the Timeline view of the My Project panel, and choose Properties. Image Size shows your frame size. Frame size is also shown in the preview area of Available Media.

For more information, see "To access the Organizer from Premiere Elements" on page 235 and "To add files from a hard drive" on page 72.

To change the default duration for still images

When you add a still image, you can assign a specific duration to it, which specifies how much time the image occupies in the Timeline. You can set a default duration for all still images that you add, and you can change their duration in the Timeline.

The frame rate of your project determines the amount of time that a certain number of frames occupies. For example, for NTSC, if you are working in a 29.97 frame-per-second (fps) project and you enter 30 frames as the duration, each still image that you add to the Timeline has a duration of about one second. For PAL, if you are working in a 25 fps project and you enter 25 frames as the duration, each still image that you add to the Timeline has a duration of one second.

1 Do one of the following:

- Choose Edit > Preferences > General.

- Click the More button in the Available Media view of the Media panel and choose Still Image Duration.

2 For Still Image Default Duration, specify the number of frames you want as a default duration.

Note: Changing the default duration of still images does not affect the duration of still images that are already in the My Project panel or in the Available Media view of the Media panel. To apply the new default length to all still images in your project, delete them from Available Media and reimport them into your project.

To set a unique duration for a still image

❖ Do one of the following:

- Position the Selection tool over either end of the image, and drag.

- Select the clip and choose Clip > Time Stretch. Enter a new duration and click OK.

To add still-image files without resizing them

1 Choose Edit > Preferences > General.

2 Deselect Default Scale To Frame Size, and click OK.

For more information, see "Adding an animation or still-image sequence," and "To add numbered still-image files and compile them into a single clip" in Adobe Premiere Elements Help.

To add files from a hard drive

- To add one or more files from your hard drive, click the Get Media From button 📷 in the task bar and select Files And Folders. Locate and select the files that you want to add, and then click Open. To add entire folders, select the items that you want to add and click Add Folder.

- To add files and folders by dragging, drag them from a desktop panel to the Media panel in Adobe Premiere Elements. If you have Photoshop Elements installed on your computer, you can drag files or copy and paste them from the Photoshop Elements Organizer to the Media panel.

For more information, see "To access the Organizer from Premiere Elements" on page 235.

To add files from DVDs, still cameras, mobile phones, tapeless camcorders, and other devices

Many types of devices other than DV camcorders record video and store still-image files. Using the Media Downloader feature, you can import these files from tapeless camcorders and mobile devices, as well as from removable media such as DVDs, memory cards, and multimedia cards. Adobe Premiere Elements copies these files to the hard drive location you specify and adds them to the Available Media view of the Media panel.

A B C

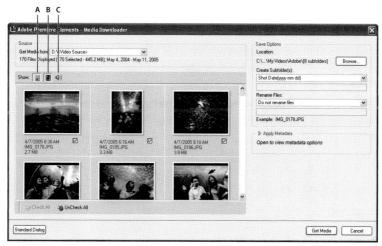

Adobe Premiere Elements - Media Downloader
A. *Show/hide image files* **B.** *Show/hide video files* **C.** *Show/hide audio files*

1 Place the DVD into your computer's DVD drive, or connect the DVD camcorder, mobile phone, or other device to your computer using the USB 2.0 port.

Note: Be sure to install any drivers required by your device. Consult the manual.

2 In the Media panel, click Get Media From 📷.

3 Click the DVD, Digital Camera, Mobile Phone, Hard Drive Camcorder, Card Reader button 📷.

4 In the Adobe Premiere Elements - Media Downloader dialog box, click the Advanced Dialog button.

5 In the Advanced Dialog box, choose the drive or device from the Get Media From pop-up menu.

Thumbnails of all importable files appear in the dialog box.

Note: When you import a DVD using Media Downloader, VOB files for menus are distinguished from video files by the word Menu, as in (Menu)VTS_01_0.VOB.

6 To specify a location for the saved files, do one of the following:

• To save files to the default Adobe folder in the My Videos folder, leave the location as it appears in the dialog box.

- To specify a different location, click Browse and choose a folder or click Make New Folder to create and name a new folder.

- To create one or more subfolders for grouping files by criteria, click the triangle next to the Create Subfolder(s) field, and choose one of the options from the pop-up menu for naming the subfolder.

- To rename the files in the folder consistently, click the triangle next to the Rename Files field, and choose one of the options from the pop-up menu for naming the files. The filename defaults to the folder name you enter. When the files are added to the folder and the Available Media view of the Media panel, the filenames are incremented by 001. For example, if you enter **summer**, the filenames are changed to summer001.vob, summer002.vob, and so on.

7 For the Show options, click the Images button ▣ , Video button ▤ , Audio button ◀◧) , or all of them.

8 Select files to add to Available Media. A check mark below the file's thumbnail indicates that the file is selected. By default, all files are selected. Click an option to remove the check mark and exclude a file. You can also select or deselect all files by using the Check All button 🐸 or the UnCheck All button 🐸 .

9 Click the triangle next to Apply Metadata, and fill in the Author and Copyright fields, if you wish.

10 Click Get Media. You can click Cancel in the Progress dialog box at any time to stop the process.

Note: *If you don't intend to use all the files you add, you can delete them from the Available Media view of the Media panel. Deleting files from the Media panel doesn't delete them from your hard drive. This practice is recommended for large VOB files.*

 For more information, see "To activate a component" in Adobe Premiere Elements Help.

For more information, see "Preparing a project for video capture" on page 52 and "To capture from DV and HDV camcorders" on page 58.

Keeping track of clips and source files

About the Available Media view of the Media panel

The Available Media view of the Media panel helps you collect, organize, and preview source material for your projects. It serves as a staging area for video and audio clips you assemble and edit in the My Project panel. After you add source files to Available Media, you can then add them to a movie by dragging them to the My Project panel.

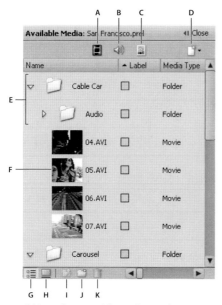

Available Media view of the Media panel
A. Show video *B. Show audio* *C. Show still images* *D. New item* *E. Folders* *F. Clip thumbnail* *G. List view*
H. Icon view *I. Move up a level* *J. New Folder* *K. Clear*

For more information, see "Methods for adding media" on page 51 and "To add files from DVDs, still cameras, mobile phones, tapeless camcorders, and other devices" on page 72.

To display and arrange media items

In the Available Media view of the Media panel, you can display items in either List view or Icon view. List view lets you view more items simultaneously and sort items by properties such as media type and duration. Icon view displays thumbnails that let you visually organize project contents.

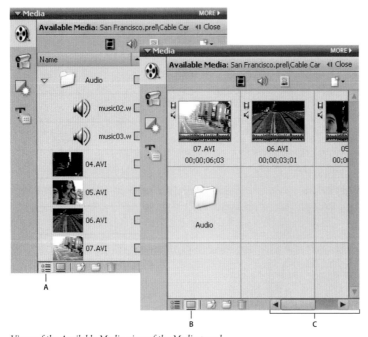

Views of the Available Media view of the Media panel
A. *Icon view* **B.** *List view* **C.** *Drag scroll bar or panel border to see more column headings in List View.*

- To change the view of Available Media, click the List View button ⊟☰ or the Icon View button ▦ at the bottom of the panel. Alternatively, click the More button, and choose View > List or View > Icon.

- To arrange items in Icon view, drag an item to any square. As you drag, a vertical bar indicates where the item is going. If you drag an item to a folder, the item goes inside the folder.

- To sort items in List view, click the column heading by which you want to sort the items. (For example, click Media Type to sort items by type.) If folders are expanded, items sort from the top level and down the Available Media view hierarchy. To reverse the sort order, click the column heading again.

- To see more of the column headings in List View, drag the right side of the Media panel to the right to resize it, or drag the scroll bar at the bottom of the panel to the right.

- To remove empty spaces between items in Icon view and arrange them within the width of the Available Media view, click the More button, and choose Clean Up.

For more information about displaying clips and their properties, see Adobe Premiere Elements Help.

For more information, see "To create a rough cut" on page 79.

To rename clips and source files

- To rename a clip, select it, choose Clip > Rename, type the new name, and press Enter. (The change affects only references used in the project; the name of the original source file in Windows remains the same.)

- To rename an original source file, close Adobe Premiere Elements, and rename the file in Windows. The next time you open the project, Adobe Premiere Elements asks you to locate the file.

You can also rename a selected clip by clicking its name once to select the text, typing the new name, and pressing Enter.

To find an item in a project

1 Choose Edit > Find.

2 Specify options according to the contents of any column in List view.

3 Click Find.

To find an item on the hard drive, select the clip, choose File > Get Properties For, and note the path at the top of the Properties panel.

For more information, see "To locate missing files" on page 40.

To delete media

Because Adobe Premiere Elements doesn't store actual media files in the project, deleting a clip from a project removes all instances from a movie but does not delete the clip's source file from the Windows desktop. To conserve disk space, also delete the source file through Windows Explorer.

- To delete a media file from a project, select it in the Available Media view of the Media panel, and press the Delete key.

- To delete a media file from both a project and your computer, select it in the Available Media view of the Media panel, and press Ctrl+Delete. Then, click OK in the Delete dialog box.

To identify unused items in a project, note the Video Usage and Audio Usage columns in List View. To display these columns, scroll to the right.

For more information, see "Creating specialty clips," "Analyzing clip properties and data rate," "Working with aspect ratios," "Working with square-pixel footage," and "Working with offline files" in Adobe Premiere Elements Help.

Chapter 5: Arranging clips

Arranging basics

About arranging clips

After you have added your media to your project, you are ready to arrange your various clips: video, still images and sounds. You can place them in an order that will tell a story, convey an impression, or communicate a thought. Adobe Premiere Elements provides many tools to help you create your movie, from a feature that helps you make slide shows from still images automatically, to markers that can help you edit video to a musical beat, and a tool that helps you place one video clip over another, picture-in-picture style.

You arrange clips in the My Project panel. It has two views: a Sceneline for basic movie editing, and a Timeline for more advanced techniques. You can switch between the two views as you edit. For example, you might arrange your clips into their correct order, narrate, create titles, place music, and place transitions in the Sceneline, then switch to the Timeline to add more soundtracks and layer clips, and trim the clips further.

For more information, see "About workspaces and panels" on page 43 and "About the Available Media view of the Media panel" on page 75.

To create a rough cut

You can arrange your clips into the desired order before dropping them into the My Project panel. This allows you to create a rough cut of a sequence very quickly. With the rough cut in place, you can move on to more detailed editing.

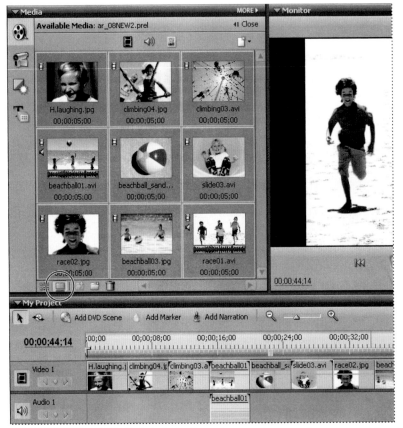

In the Icon view of Available Media in the Media panel, arrange images or clips as you want them to appear in the movie.

1 Click the Available Media button in the Media panel.

2 Click the Icon view button in the Media panel.

This shows all your media in a grid.

3 In the Media panel, drag your clips into the desired order.

4 Click the More button at the upper right of the Media panel.

5 Select Clean Up from the pop-up menu.

This removes empty spaces from the grid.

6 Make sure no clips are selected in the Media panel. Then, choose Edit > Select All.

7 Click the Timeline button 🖳 in the My Project panel.

8 Place the current-time indicator 🖐 at the spot in the Timeline where you want the sequence to begin.

9 Do one of the following:

• Choose Clip > Insert to insert the sequence into the Timeline before clips to the right of the current-time indicator.

• Choose Clip > Overlay to replace clips already in the Timeline to the right of the current-time indicator.

A rough cut of your sequence appears in the Timeline.

Note: *You can also choose Clip > Insert and Clip > Overlay to place the rough cut at a selected target area in the Sceneline.*

For more information, see "Using the Sceneline view of the My Project panel" on page 81.

Arranging clips in the Sceneline

Using the Sceneline view of the My Project panel

The Sceneline view of the My Project panel provides a stage on which you can arrange your clips into a movie. In the Sceneline, each clip is represented by its first frame. This display makes it easy to arrange clips into coherent sequences without regard for clip length. This technique is sometimes referred to as *storyboard-style editing*. The Sceneline shows a Scenes video track where you place video clips and other images, a Narration soundtrack for any narrations you might record, and a soundtrack where you can place background music and other sounds. In the Sceneline, you can also add titles, transitions, special effects, and DVD scene markers. Use the Sceneline to assemble your movie quickly and easily. For more advanced editing, use the Timeline.

Sceneline view of the My Project panel

Using the Sceneline, you can easily insert a clip before another, after another, or even split it before inserting it.

For more information, see "About workspaces and panels" on page 43 and "About creating titles" on page 151.

To place a clip in the Sceneline

1 Click the Sceneline button ⬛⬜⬜ in the My Project panel.

2 Click the Available Media button 🎞 in the Media panel.

3 Drag the clip from the Media panel to one of the empty clip targets in the Sceneline. When the pointer turns into the insert icon 📥, release the mouse button.

For more information, see "To insert a clip before another in the Sceneline" on page 82 and "About the Timeline" on page 88.

To insert a clip before another in the Sceneline

1 Click the Sceneline button ⬛⬜⬜ in the My Project panel.

2 Click the Available Media button 🎞 in the Media panel.

3 Drag the clip from Available Media onto the clip in the Sceneline.

The new clip appears in front of the one on which you dropped it and all subsequent clips shift to the right.

For more information, see "To place a clip in the Sceneline" on page 82.

To insert a clip after another in the Sceneline

1 Click the Sceneline button ▣▢▢ in the My Project panel.

2 Click the Available Media button 🎞 in the Media panel.

3 In the Sceneline view of the My Project panel, select the clip after which you want to insert the new clip.

4 Drag the clip from Available Media and drop it onto the Monitor.

The new clip appears to the right of the selected clip, and subsequent clips shift to the right.

For more information, see "To insert a clip before another in the Sceneline" on page 82.

To insert one clip into another in the Sceneline

You can quickly split one clip into two pieces and insert another clip into the split.

1 In the Media panel, click the Available Media button 🎞 .

2 In the My Project panel, click the Sceneline button ▣▢▢ .

3 In the Sceneline, select the clip to be split.

4 In the Monitor panel, drag the current-time indicator ▽ to the frame where you want to make the split.

5 Shift-drag a clip from Available Media and drop it onto the Monitor panel.

6 Select Split And Insert.

Adobe Premiere Elements will split the first clip and insert the second into the split.

To move a clip in the Sceneline

1 Click the Sceneline button ▣▢▢ in the My Project panel.

2 Shift-drag a clip from a location in the Sceneline to another location before or after another clip. A vertical blue line shows the target area and the pointer changes to the insert icon ▶☐ .

3 Release the mouse button.

4 Choose one of the following:

Move Scene And Its Objects Moves the clip with any overlays it might have, such as a title.

Move Just Scene Moves the clip without overlays.

The clip moves to its new location and all subsequent clips shift to the right.

To delete a clip in the Sceneline

1 Click the Sceneline button ▣▣▣ in the My Project panel.

2 Select a clip in the Sceneline.

3 Press Shift-Delete.

4 Choose one of the following:

Delete Scene And Its Objects Deletes the clip and any overlays it might have, such as a title.

Delete Just Scene Deletes the clip but leaves overlays.

The clip leaves the Sceneline.

To create a Picture In Picture overlay

You can place one video clip in a small frame over a background video clip that covers the entire screen. This effect is called a Picture In Picture overlay.

Picture in Picture overlay

1 Click the Sceneline button ⬛⬜⬛ in the My Project panel.

2 Select the clip in the Sceneline that you want to use as the background clip.

The selected clip appears in the Monitor.

3 Click the Available Media button 🎞 in the Media panel.

4 Shift-drag a clip from the Media panel onto a spot on the clip in the Monitor panel.

5 Select Picture In Picture.

The clip you dragged appears in a frame at the chosen location, superimposed on the background clip.

6 To adjust the position of the superimposed clip, drag it to the desired location in the Monitor.

Note: If the superimposed clip is longer than the background clip, it appears over successive clips in the Sceneline for its entire duration, and appears superimposed over those clips during playback.

For more information, see "To delete a Picture In Picture overlay" on page 86.

To delete a Picture In Picture overlay

1 Click the Sceneline button ▣▣▢ in the My Project panel.

2 Select the superimposed clip in the Monitor panel.

3 Right-click the lavender clip representation in the mini-timeline of the Monitor panel.

4 Select Delete.

The superimposed clip disappears from the Sceneline and the Monitor.

For more information, see "To create a Picture In Picture overlay" on page 84.

To create a slide show

You can create a slide show from a collection of still images very easily using the Sceneline.

Note: If you have Photoshop Elements, you can add clips from the Organizer to the Adobe Premiere Elements My Project panel by dragging, copying, and pasting. (See "To access the Organizer from Premiere Elements" on page 235.)

1 Click the Available Media button 🎞 in the Media panel.

2 Click the Show Still Images 🖼 button at the top right of Available Media, and deselect the Show Video button 🎞 and Show Audio 🔊 button.

3 Click the Sceneline button ▣▣▢ in the My Project panel.

4 In the Media panel, Ctrl-click still images in the order in which you want them to appear in the slide show.

5 Drag the selected group to a target area in the Sceneline.

6 Choose one of the following:

Add As Individual Stills This option places each still image onto its own target area in the Sceneline.

Add As Grouped Slideshow This option places the entire group onto one target that can be moved as a single clip.

The Create Slideshow dialog box will appear.

7 In the Create Slideshow dialog box, select the options desired and click OK.

A grouped slide show clip is created in the selected target area of the Sceneline. A slideshow icon ![icon] appears to the upper right of the grouped slide show clip.

For more information, see "To expand or close grouped slide shows" on page 87.

To expand or close grouped slide shows
❖ In the Sceneline, click the Expand/Close strip to the right of the clip.

Grouped slideshow in the Sceneline. The Expand/Close strip shows or hides all slides in the group.

This expands the grouped slide show, displaying its still images in sequence, or closes the slide show so that it appears as a single clip with only its first image displayed.

For more information, see "To create a slide show" on page 86.

To ungroup a slide show
You can convert a grouped slide show clip into a simple series of still images in the My Project panel.

1 In the My Project panel, click the Sceneline button ![icon] .

2 Right-click a grouped slideshow clip in the Sceneline.

3 Select Ungroup Scenes.

Each still photo from the grouped slide show will appear in its own target area in the Sceneline.

Understanding the Timeline

About the Timeline

The Timeline view of the My Project panel graphically represents your movie project as video and audio clips arranged in vertically stacked tracks. When you capture video from a digital video device, the clips appear sequentially as they occur in the My Project panel. Typically, when editing a movie, you initially create a rough cut—a complete but relatively crude version of the movie. The Timeline view of the My Project panel uses a time ruler to display the components of your movie and their relationship to each other over time. You can trim and add scenes, indicate important frames with markers, add transitions, and control how clips are blended or superimposed.

The zoom controls in the Timeline allow you to zoom out to see your entire video, or zoom in to see clips in more detail. You can also change how the clips appear in the tracks, and resize the tracks and the header area.

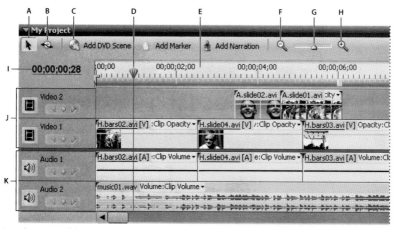

Timeline view of the My Project panel
A. *Selection tool* **B.** *Time Stretch tool* **C.** *Add DVD Scene* **D.** *Current-time indicator* **E.** *Time ruler* **F.** *Zoom controls* **G.** *Timecode* **H.** *Video tracks* **I.** *Audio tracks*

By default the Timeline contains three tracks for video and still images, and five tracks for audio, including one each for narration and background music. When you drag clips that include both audio and video (called *linked clips*) to a track, the video and audio components appear separately in their respective tracks. A typical clip might include both an audio and a video track.

Tracks let you layer your video or audio, and you can add additional tracks at any time. With multiple video tracks, you can add compositing effects, picture-in-picture effects, overlay titles, and more. With multiple audio tracks, you can add a narration to one track and background music to another track. The final movie combines all the video and audio tracks.

Adobe Premiere Elements automatically inserts a new track if you drag and release a clip above the topmost video track or below the bottommost audio track. At times you may want to insert and name tracks before you begin adding clips. You can add or delete tracks at any time and specify a name for each one. The number of tracks a project can contain has no limit. A movie must contain at least one of each type of track (although the track can be empty). New video tracks appear above existing video tracks, and new audio tracks appear below existing audio tracks. The video track order is important because any clip located in Video 2 also overlays the Video 1 track. Below the Video 1 track are the Audio 1 and Audio 2 tracks. These audio tracks are combined in playback and the track order is not relevant.

You can specify the default number and type of tracks in new movies.

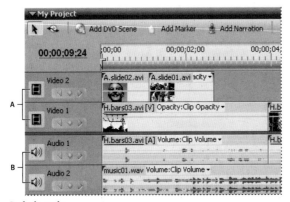

Default tracks
A. *Video tracks* **B.** *Audio tracks*

For more information, see "Using the Sceneline view of the My Project panel" on page 81.

Editing tools in the Timeline

You use the tools in the upper left corner of the Timeline view of the My Project panel to trim clips and change their speed, add markers, or add narration. When you edit in the Timeline, the pointer changes to the currently active tool. If the pointer changes to a red slash, you cannot use the tool on the clip underneath the pointer.

Selection tool ⟩ Selects clips for previewing or trimming.

Time Stretch tool ⟲ Changes the playback speed and duration of a clip without changing its In or Out points. Dragging the edge of a clip in one direction lengthens it and slows it down; dragging it in the other direction shortens the clip and speeds it up.

Add DVD Scene tool ⟳ Adds any of three types of DVD markers into the Timeline at the location of the current-time indicator.

Add Marker tool 🔖 Adds an unnumbered marker to the Timeline at the location of the current-time indicator.

Add Narration tool 🎤 Opens the Record Voice Narration panel, which holds tools for recording voice-overs.

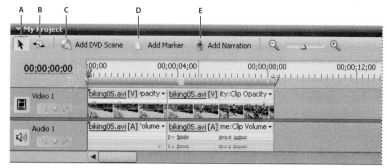

Editing tools in the Timeline view of the My Project panel
A. Selection B. Time Stretch C. Add DVD Scene D. Add Marker E. Add Narration

Note: *Both the Add DVD Scene tool and the Add Narration tool are located in the upper left of the Sceneline, as well as in the Timeline.*

For more information, see "To trim clips in the Timeline" on page 106 and "To change a clip's speed by using the Time Stretch tool" on page 113.

Moving through the Timeline

In the time ruler of the Timeline, the current-time indicator corresponds to the frame displayed in the Monitor. A vertical line extends from this current-time indicator through all the tracks. The time display in the upper left corner indicates the current time using the timecode format of hours;minutes;seconds;frames (for NTSC drop-frame format video) or hours:minutes:seconds:frames (for NTSC non-drop-frame format video and PAL format video).

For information about changing the timecode used in the My Project panel (and throughout the project), see "General settings" in Adobe Premiere Elements Help.

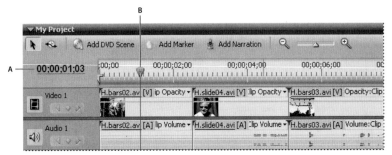

Time navigation controls in the Timeline view of the My Project panel
A. Time display showing position of current-time indicator **B.** *Current-time indicator*

To position the current-time indicator

1 In the My Project panel, click the Timeline button 🖳 .

2 In the Timeline, do any of the following.

- Drag the current-time indicator 🖐 .

- Click the time ruler where you want to position the current-time indicator.

- Press Shift while dragging the current-time indicator to snap it to the edge of the closest clip or marker.

- Drag the time display (to the left of the time ruler) to the desired time value.

- Click the time display (to the left of the time ruler), type a valid time, and then press Enter. (You don't need to type leading zeros, colons, or semicolons. However, be aware that Adobe Premiere Elements interprets numbers under 100 as frames.)

💡 *You can use the Home or End keys on the keyboard to skip back to the beginning or ahead to the end of the movie. The Page Up and Page Down keys go to the previous and next clips. The Right or Left Arrow keys move the current-time indicator forward or back a frame, while pressing Shift+Right Arrow or Shift+Left Arrow moves it in increments of five frames.*

To zoom in or out of the Timeline time ruler

When you zoom in on the Timeline, Adobe Premiere Elements magnifies the Timeline around the current-time indicator, letting you examine smaller increments of media. You can also zoom in as you add a clip to the Timeline, magnifying the location around the pointer rather than the current-time indicator. This technique lets you see the exact placement of the insertion point before you release the mouse. In contrast, zooming out shows more of the Timeline, giving you a visual summary of the movie.

1 Click the Timeline button 🖳 in the My Project panel.

2 Do one of the following:

- To zoom in or out as you add a clip, drag a clip to the Timeline. Hold down the mouse button and press the Equals (=) key to increase the zoom factor or press the Minus (–) key to decrease it.

- To zoom in on the Timeline, drag the Zoom slider to the right, or click the Zoom In button 🔍 .

- To zoom out of the Timeline, drag the Zoom slider to the left, or click the Zoom Out button 🔍 .

💡 *To zoom out so that the entire length of the movie is visible in the Timeline, make sure that the Timeline view of the My Project panel is active, and then press the Backslash (\) key. You can also zoom in and out by pressing the Equals (=) or Minus (-) keys on the keyboard (not the numeric keypad).*

❓ *For more information about working with tracks and arranging clips in the Timeline, see Adobe Premiere Elements Help.*

Previewing movies

Previewing a movie in the Monitor panel

You can preview all or part of a movie at any time in the Monitor panel. To preview a movie, Adobe Premiere Elements must first prepare the clips on all the tracks for viewing, applying effects, motion, opacity, and volume settings. Adobe Premiere Elements dynamically adjusts video quality and frame rate in order to preview the movie in real time. Movies that use only cuts between clips generally preview at normal quality and frame rate.

More complex movies (with effects and layered video and audio), require more processing time to display properly. If Adobe Premiere Elements can't display an area at full speed and quality, it adds a thin, red line in the time ruler of the Timeline. To preview one of these areas, you can first *render* it. Rendering processes the layers and effects and saves the resultant preview into a file, which Adobe Premiere Elements can use each time you preview that section of the movie. Once rendered, a section doesn't require rerendering, unless changes are made to it. (In the Timeline, rendered areas are marked with a green line.)

Note: *If you make significant changes to a rendered area, the preview file is no longer useful, and the green line turns red. To preview complex effects at the full frame rate, you'll have to rerender the area.*

You designate the area to render by using the *work area bar* in the Timeline.

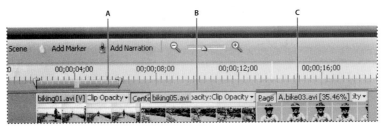

Timeline
*A. Work area bar **B.** Green bar indicates fully rendered area **C.** Red bar indicates area needs rendering for best quality preview*

Using the controls in the Monitor panel, you can resize the video pane, jump to various frames, or play the clip fullscreen.

When using the Sceneline view of the My Project panel, you can also zoom in and out of the *mini-timeline* that appears in the Monitor panel to expand or contract its increments. Zooming in on the mini-timeline helps you see changes happening over small expanses of time, even over the duration of a single frame. Zooming out helps you see changes happening over longer spans.

Monitor panel
A. *Add Text* ***B.*** *Freeze Frame* ***C.*** *Play Full Screen* ***D.*** *Mini-timeline* ***E.*** *Current Time* ***F.*** *Go To Beginning of Movie* ***G.*** *Zoom to Timeline* ***H.*** *Playback controls* ***I.*** *Split Clip* ***J.*** *Clip duration*

You can preview a movie or clip full-screen, to get an idea of how it would appear on a television screen. Also, this makes it easier to share your work with others in the room.

For more information on preview files, see "Understanding preview files" and "Deleting preview files" in Help.

For more information, see "To set the area to be rendered" on page 97 and "To render a preview" on page 98.

To preview a movie

- To preview in the Timeline, click the Play button ▶.

- To preview when the Timeline is active, press the spacebar.

- To preview in the Sceneline, double-click the clip in the Sceneline.

- To control the speed of the preview, drag the shuttle slider to the right in the Monitor panel. The clip plays faster the further you drag the shuttle slider.

- To play in reverse, drag the shuttle slider to the left in the Monitor panel. The clip rewinds faster the further you drag the shuttle slider.

- To pause the preview, click the Pause button ▮▮ in the Monitor or press the spacebar. (The Play button and the spacebar toggle between Play and Pause.)

- To go forward one frame, click the Frame Forward button ▮▶ in the Monitor panel.

- To go forward five frames, Shift-click the Frame Forward button in the Monitor panel.

- To go backward one frame, click the Frame Back button ◀▮ in the Monitor panel.

- To go backward five frames, Shift-click the Frame Back button in the Monitor panel.

- To jump to a different frame, click the current-time display, and type the new time. (You don't need to type colons or semicolons. However, be aware that Adobe Premiere Elements interprets numbers under 100 as frames.)

- To go to the end of the previous clip (the cut or edit point), click the Go To Previous Edit Point button ◀◀▮ in the Monitor panel.

- To go to the beginning of the next clip, click the Go To Next Edit Point button ▮▶▶ in the Monitor panel.

For information about controlling playback in the Timeline, see "To scroll the Timeline during preview" in Adobe Premiere Elements Help.

- To preview a movie in full-screen mode, click the Play Full Screen button 🖥 in the Monitor.

About previewing in full-screen mode

To see the greatest detail in a clip or movie, preview it in full-screen mode. This mode fills the computer screen with video, suggesting how clips and movies will appear on TV screens.

To preview in full-screen mode

❖ In the Monitor panel, click the Play Full Screen button 🖥. The preview pane fills the screen, and playback starts automatically.

To pause, reverse, and advance a full-screen preview

In addition to playing and pausing a full-screen preview, you can reverse or advance in single-frame increments.

1 To display the control bar, move the cursor to the bottom of the screen.

In full-screen preview, move the cursor across the screen to display the player controls.

2 Click the Pause ⏸ , Frame Back ◀ , or Frame Forward ▶ buttons.

To exit full-screen mode

1 To display the control bar, move the cursor to the bottom of the screen.

2 To the right of the control bar, click Exit.

To set the area to be rendered

• Drag the textured center of the work area bar over the section you want to preview. Make sure that you drag the work area bar from its center; otherwise you move the current-time indicator instead.

Grabbing the work area bar and dragging it over a section to preview

- If the textured center is not visible, Alt-drag the work area bar over the section you want to preview.

Dragging a work area marker to mark the end of the work area

- Position the current-time indicator, and press Alt+[to set the beginning of the work area.
- Position the current-time indicator, and press Alt+] to set the end of the work area.
- Alt-double-click the work area bar to resize it to the width of the movie.
- Double-click the work area bar to resize it to the width of the time ruler, or the length of the entire movie, whichever is shorter.

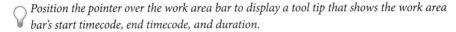 *Position the pointer over the work area bar to display a tool tip that shows the work area bar's start timecode, end timecode, and duration.*

To render a preview

❖ Set the work area bar over the area you want to preview, and choose Timeline > Render Work Area. (The rendering time depends on your system's resources and the complexity of the segment.)

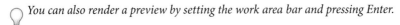 *You can also render a preview by setting the work area bar and pressing Enter.*

Chapter 6: Editing clips

Clip editing basics

Clip editing methods

The process of editing clips includes previewing and trimming them to eliminate unnecessary material. It could also include revising clip properties such as speed, direction, and duration. If you have media clips generated by other programs, you can also edit them in their original applications from within Adobe Premiere Elements.

About trimming clips

There are several ways to build a movie, but all of them involve selecting the portions of source clips you want to include. You rarely use an entire clip. *In* and *Out* points define the first and last frames you want to use from a clip. Setting In and Out points does not actually delete frames from the hard drive, but instead isolates the portion of the clip you want included in the movie. In a manner of speaking, In and Out points open a window over the clip, showing only the part you select. You can move them as needed to regain any frames you might have trimmed off.

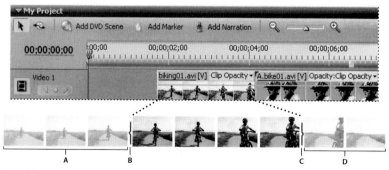

In and Out points serve as a window over a clip
A. *Trimmed frames* **B.** *In point* **C.** *Out point* **D.** *Trimmed frames*

You always trim from either end of a clip. To trim frames from the middle of a clip, you must first split the clip (which creates two instances of the original clip), and then trim the unwanted frames from the end of the first new clip or the beginning of the second. You can trim a clip by clicking buttons in the Preview window, by dragging handles in the Monitor panel while viewing the Sceneline, or by dragging the ends of the clip in the Timeline.

For more information, see "Splitting clips" on page 109.

Trimming clips in the Preview window

About trimming in the Preview window

You can preview any clip and set new In and Out points for it before arranging it with others in the My Project panel. You might, for example, preview your clips to determine their quality and trim off their unusable parts before starting to arrange them. You can preview and trim clips in the Preview window.

Trimming a clip in the Preview window sets its In and Out points for all subsequent instances placed in the My Project panel. It does not change the In and Out points of instances of the clip that are already in the My Project panel.

Preview window
A. Zoom control B. Clip in point C. Current time D. Current-time indicator E. Playback controls F. Clip out point G. Clip duration

For more information, see "About workspaces and panels" on page 43.

To preview a clip in the Preview window

1 Click the Available Media button 🎞 in the Media panel.

2 Double-click a clip in Available Media.

3 Do any of the following in the Preview window:

• To play the clip, click the Play button 🔘 .

• To step back or forward one frame, click the Step Back button 🔘 or the Step Forward button 🔘 .

• To step back or forward five frames, Shift-click the Step Back button 🔘 or the Step Forward button 🔘 .

For more information, see "About the Available Media view of the Media panel" on page 75 and "To preview a movie" on page 95.

To trim a clip in the Preview window

You can trim a clip in the Preview window before placing it in the My Project panel. The Set In and Set Out buttons mark the start and end frames of the clip. Once a clip is in a movie, you can reopen it in the Preview window to change its In and Out points for subsequent instances, either regaining frames previously trimmed or trimming additional frames.

1 Click the Available Media button ⊕ in the Media panel.

2 Double-click a clip in Available Media.

3 To trim the clip, do any of the following in the Preview window:

- To set a new In point, either drag the In point handle ▯ to the desired location, or drag the current-time indicator ▽ to the desired location and click the Set In button ▯.

- To set a new Out point, either drag the Out point handle ◢ to the desired location, or drag the current-time indicator ▽ to the desired location and click the Set Out button ◢.

4 Click the Close button ✖ in the Preview window.

Subsequent instances of the clip dragged from Available Media will assume the In and Out points of the trimmed clip. Trimming in the Preview window does not affect instances of the clip that are already in the My Project panel.

For more information, see "To trim a clip in the Monitor panel" on page 103 and "To trim clips in the Timeline" on page 106.

To zoom in and out in the Preview window

When previewing a clip in the Preview window, you can zoom in or out of its *mini-timeline* to expand or contract its increments. Zooming in on the mini-timeline helps you see changes happening over small expanses of time, even over the duration of a single frame. Zooming out helps you see changes happening over longer spans.

- To zoom in, drag the Zoom Claw ▭ at the left of the zoom control toward the right of the Monitor panel. Alternately, drag the Zoom Claw at the right of the zoom control toward the left.

- To zoom out, drag the Zoom Claw ▭ at the left of the zoom control toward the left of the Monitor panel. Alternately, drag the Zoom Claw at the right of the zoom control toward the right.

Trimming clips in the Sceneline

To trim a clip in the Monitor panel

When the My Project panel displays the Sceneline, you can trim clips directly in the Monitor panel.

1 In the My Project panel, click the Sceneline button ▮▯▮ .

2 Select a clip in the Sceneline.

The clip will appear in the Monitor panel, with a clip representation containing the clip's file name in the mini-timeline.

3 Do one of the following:

- To trim the clip from the beginning, drag the In point handle ▮ (on the left of the clip representation) to the right.

- To trim the clip from the end, drag the Out point handle▮ (on the right of the clip representation) to the left.

The Monitor panel shows the frame at the location of the handle you dragged.

For more information, see "Using the Sceneline view of the My Project panel" on page 81 and "To trim clips in the Timeline" on page 106.

To remove frames from the middle of a clip in the Sceneline

You may want to retain material at the beginning and end of a clip for your movie, but remove the material from its middle. You can split the clip right before the unwanted section begins, creating two clips; then you can trim the unwanted material from the beginning of the second clip.

1 In the My Project panel, click the Sceneline button ▮▯▮ .

2 In the Sceneline, select the clip containing unwanted material.

The clip appears in the Monitor panel, with a clip representation containing its file name in the mini-timeline.

3 Drag the current-time indicator in the Monitor panel to the frame where the unwanted material begins.

4 In the Monitor panel, click the Split Clip button ▮ .

Two clip representations replace the original in both the mini-timeline and the Sceneline.

5 Select the representation of the second clip in the mini-timeline.

6 Drag the Set In handle ![handle] of the clip representation to the right until it is past the unwanted material.

In the mini-timeline, drag the Set In handle to trim frames from the beginning of a clip.

The unwanted material is removed from the beginning of the second clip, and the gap created between the first and second clips is automatically closed.

> *For more information, see "To zoom in and out of the Monitor panel mini-timeline" in Adobe Premiere Elements Help.*

For more information, see "To remove frames from the middle of a clip in the Timeline" on page 107 and "About splitting clips" on page 109.

Trimming clips in the Timeline

About trimming clips in the Timeline

You can remove or regain trimmed frames from either end of a clip by dragging the clip's edge in the Timeline view of the My Project panel. To help you locate the precise frame you want, the Monitor panel displays the frame at the changing In or Out point of the clip as you drag. If a clip has another clip immediately adjacent to the edge you're trimming, the Monitor panel displays the frames of both clips side-by-side. The frame on the left (the Out point) is earlier in time, and the frame on the right (the In point) is later in time. Subsequent clips in the Timeline shift as you drag the clip's edge. When trimming frames, empty space adjacent to the edge you trim shifts in time just as a clip would.

A tool tip displays the number of frames you are trimming as you trim them. This window displays a negative value if you drag the edge toward the beginning of the movie and a positive number if you drag toward the end of the movie. You can tell whether you have trimmed a clip by looking for a small gray triangle in the top corner at either end of the clip in the Timeline. The triangle indicates you have not trimmed that edge.

The Timeline during (above) and after (below) trimming. Gray triangle in corner of clip disappears when you trim.

For linked clips (video that includes a soundtrack), dragging the edge of one, changes the In or Out points of both clips. Sometimes you want to trim linked clips independently in order to create split edits (also known as L-cuts and J-cuts). Pressing Alt when you trim allows you set the In and Out points of the video and audio separately. (See "To extend audio before or after linked video" in Adobe Premiere Elements Help.)

For more information, see "Editing tools in the Timeline" on page 90 and "To trim a clip in the Preview window" on page 102.

To trim clips in the Timeline

1 In the My Project panel, click Timeline 🖼 .

2 Click the Selection tool ▶ .

To trim only one clip of a linked pair, Alt-select the clip to temporarily unlink them. Select them again to move them as a unit.

3 Position the pointer over the edge of the clip you want to trim until the correct icon appears:

- Trim-In icon ◀▶ to trim the beginning of a clip.

- Trim-Out icon ◀▶ to trim the end of a clip.

4 Drag the edge to the desired frame. Notice that the Monitor panel displays the frames as you drag, also showing the frame from the adjacent clip (if any). Subsequent clips in the track shift in time to compensate for the edit, but their durations remain unchanged.

Note: You cannot drag the In point of a clip to the left past the edge of an adjacent clip.

For information on how to retrieve trimmed frames, see "Retrieving trimmed frames" in Adobe Premiere Elements Help.

For information on trimming in the Monitor panel, see "To trim a clip in the Monitor panel" in Adobe Premiere Elements Help.

For more information, see "To zoom in or out of the Timeline time ruler" on page 92 and "To trim a clip in the Monitor panel" on page 103.

To remove frames from the middle of a clip in the Timeline

You may want to retain material at the beginning and end of a clip for your movie, but remove the material from its middle. You can split the clip right before the unwanted section begins, then trim the unwanted material from the beginning of the second clip resulting from the split.

1 In the My Project panel, click the Timeline button .

2 In the Timeline, drag the current-time indicator to the frame where the unwanted section of a clip begins.

The frame appears in the Monitor.

3 In the Monitor, click the Split Clip button .

This will split the clip at the point selected.

4 Click the Selection tool .

5 Double-click the clip to the right of the split. This will open the clip in the Preview monitor.

6 In the Preview monitor, drag the current-time indicator to the frame just after the last frame of unwanted material.

7 Click the Set In Point button . This will trim the unwanted material from the beginning of the second clip and will shorten the clip in the Timeline, leaving a gap between it and the clip before.

Clip is split (top), In point is set (middle), Resulting gap (bottom)

8 Right-click in the gap in the Timeline, then click Delete And Close Gap.

For more information, see "To extend audio before or after linked video" in Adobe Premiere Elements Help.

For more information, see "To remove frames from the middle of a clip in the Sceneline" on page 103.

Splitting clips

About splitting clips

At times you may want to apply different effects to different parts of a clip, for example, to speed up the first part of it while leaving the second part at normal speed. To do this, you cut a clip into separate pieces, and then apply effects and transitions to those pieces. You can split a clip in a movie by using the Split Clip tool in the Monitor panel. It cuts one or more selected clips at the current-time indicator.

Splitting a clip creates a new and separate instance of the original clip, and if linked to another clip, a new instance of the linked clip as well. The resulting clips are full versions of the original clip, but with the In or Out point changed to match the location marked by the tool. You can select and delete these clips.

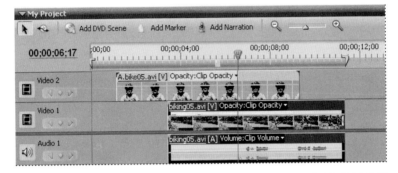

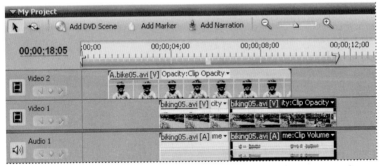

Split Clip tool (before, above and after, below) cuts selected clips at the current-time indicator.

Note: *If you want to change effect settings over time, you don't have to split the clip. You can apply keyframes to a single clip instead. (See "About keyframes" on page 143.)*

For more information, see "About trimming clips in the Timeline" on page 105 and "To trim clips in the Timeline" on page 106.

To split a clip

You can split a clip at any frame, creating one clip that ends, and another that begins, at that frame. You can edit the two resulting clips as you would any other clips.

1 In the My Project panel, click either the Sceneline button ▮▯▯ or the Timeline button 🗐 , and select a clip in the Sceneline or Timeline.

2 Do one of the following:

- If you chose Sceneline, drag the current-time indicator ⊤ in the mini-timeline of the Monitor panel to the frame where you want to create the split.

- If you chose Timeline, drag the current-time indicator ♥ in the Timeline to the frame where you want to create the split.

3 In the Monitor panel, click the Split Clip button 🗐 .

Two new clips take the place of the original clip in the My Project panel, one ending and one beginning at the location of the current-time indicator.

Retrieving trimmed frames

About retrieving trimmed frames

When you trim frames from a clip, you're actually just setting an In or Out point, which indicates the portion of the original clip that you want in the movie. All trimmed frames remain available. You can regain any frames you trim by resetting the In or Out points.

You cannot use the Preview window to retrieve frames for a clip already in the Timeline and touching other clips at its beginning and end. To use the Preview window, you must first open a space before or after the clip in the Timeline. You can, however, retrieve frames for a clip by dragging either of its ends in the Timeline. This pushes adjacent clips over to make room for the previously trimmed frames.

If you've trimmed frames from the source clip (the original clip in the Available Media view of the Media panel, not an instance of the clip in the Timeline), you can clear the In and Out points by using one of the Clear Clip Marker commands in the Clip menu. However, changes you make to the source clip do not affect instances of the clip that you've already placed in the Timeline.

For information about retrieving trimmed frames in the Timeline, see Adobe Premiere Elements Help.

To retrieve frames in the Preview window

1 In the Media panel, click the Available Media button 🎞️ .

2 Double-click the video clip in Available Media.

3 In the Preview window, do one of the following:

• Move the current-time indicator ⵜ to the frame you want as the first frame of the clip, even if it's to the left of the current in point. Click the Set In Point button 🔖 .

• Move the current-time indicator ⵜ to the frame you want as the last frame of the clip, even if it's to the right of the current out point. Click the Set Out Point button ◢ .

For more information, see "About trimming in the Preview window" on page 100.

To retrieve frames in the Sceneline

1 In the My Project panel, click the Sceneline button ◗◻◻ .

2 Select a clip in the Sceneline.

The file name for the clip, and its in and out points becomes visible in the mini-timeline of the Monitor panel.

3 In the mini-timeline of the Monitor panel, do one of the following:

• To retrieve frames at the beginning of the clip, drag the Set In handle 🔖 to the left.

• To retrieve frames at the end of the clip, drag the Set Out handle ◢ to the right.

For more information, see "To trim a clip in the Monitor panel" on page 103.

Changing clip speed, duration, and direction

Changing a clip's speed

Changing clip speed changes the clip's duration. Speeding up a clip removes frames, thus shortening the clip duration. In the same way, slowing down a clip repeats frames and thus adds to the length of a clip. For audio clips, a change in speed also changes pitch. The Time Stretch command includes an option to maintain the original pitch of an audio clip at any speed.

Note: When you change the speed of a clip containing interlaced fields, you may need to adjust how Adobe Premiere Elements treats the fields, especially when the speed drops below 100% of the original speed. (See "Processing interlaced video fields" in Adobe Premiere Elements Help.

To change a clip's speed by using the Time Stretch tool

1 In the My Project panel, click Timeline 🖿 .

2 If you plan to slow down the clip, first drag it to the end of the movie or to another track with empty space, so you can stretch it without bumping into an adjacent clip. When slowing down a clip with the Time Stretch tool, you cannot stretch it past the edge of an adjacent clip.

3 Click the Time Stretch tool 🔄 in the upper left corner of the Timeline.

4 Position the pointer over the edge of the clip you want to change until the correct icon appears:

• Time Stretch In icon ⁺⤵ to time stretch the clip to the right of the pointer.

• Time Stretch Out icon ⤴⁺ to time stretch the clip to the left of the pointer.

5 Drag the edge of the clip, increasing its length to slow it down, or shortening it to speed it up.

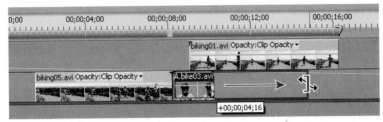

Changing clip speed by using the Time Stretch tool

6 Preview your changes, and then make adjustments as necessary. (See "To preview a movie" on page 95.)

7 If you moved the clip in step 1, click the Selection tool, and then drag the clip back into place in the movie.

To change a clip's speed by using the Time Stretch command

1 In the My Project panel, click Timeline 📇 .

2 If you plan to slow down a clip that has another clip on its right in the Timeline, drag it to an empty track or to the end of the movie so you can stretch it without bumping into an adjacent clip.

3 Select the clip in the Timeline.

Note: If you haven't yet added the clip to the Timeline, you can select it in the Available Media view of the Media panel instead.

4 Choose Clip > Time Stretch.

5 In the Time Stretch dialog box, type a percentage for Speed. A value less the 100% slows the clip down; a value greater than 100% increases its speed.

6 (Optional) To keep the pitch of an audio clip unchanged, select Maintain Audio Pitch.

7 Click OK.

Preview your changes, and then make adjustments as necessary. (See "To preview a movie" on page 95)

8 If you moved the clip in step 1, drag it back into place in the movie.

For more information, see "To set the duration of a clip" in Adobe Premiere Elements Help.

To reverse the playback of a clip

Reversing a clip plays the clip backwards, Out point to In point. You can also both reverse the clip and change its speed.

1 Select the clip in the Timeline.

2 Choose Clip > Time Stretch.

3 (Optional) To change the speed of the clip, type a percentage for Speed in the Time Stretch dialog box. A value less the 100% slows the clip down; a value greater than 100% increases its speed.

4 Select Reverse Speed, and click OK.

To both reverse the clip and change its speed with one action, type a negative percentage for Speed, where –200 plays the clip in reverse at double its normal speed and –50 plays the clip in reverse at half its normal speed.

Freezing and holding frames

About freezing and holding frames

Occasionally, you may want to capture a single frame from a video clip, to use as a still image somewhere in the movie. For example, you may want to show a character start an action, but then stop mid-action, frozen on the screen. To do this, you identify and grab a *freeze frame*.

At other times, however, you may want to *hold* a single still frame on the screen for the duration of a clip, while letting its sound track play normally. To do this, use the Frame Hold feature.

To freeze a video frame

Using the Freeze Frame button, you can grab a frame to be used as a still image from any video clip.

1 In the My Project panel, click either the Sceneline button ▣▣▣ or the Timeline button ▣ , and select a clip in the Sceneline or Timeline.

2 Do one of the following:

- If you chose Sceneline, drag the current-time indicator ⊤ in the mini-timeline of the Monitor panel to the frame you want to grab.

- If you chose Timeline, drag the current-time indicator ♈ in the Timeline to the frame you want to grab.

The Monitor panel shows the frame at the location of the current-time indicator.

3 In the Monitor panel, click the Freeze Frame button 🔳 .

The frame appears in the Freeze Frame window.

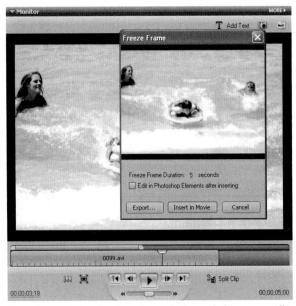

Freeze Frame window showing a frame of video ready for use as a still image

4 Do one of the following:

- To export the frame as a still image file, click Export. In the Export Frame dialog box, give the image file a name and location, then click Save.

- To insert the frame as a still image directly into the movie at the current-time indicator, click Insert In Movie.

To hold a video frame

You can hold one frame of a clip so that only that frame appears for the duration of the clip. You can hold on the clip's In point, Out point, or at a frame you designate with Marker 0 (zero) within the clip. If the video includes linked audio, the audio still plays for the duration of the clip. You can delete the audio or disable it if desired.

If you want the video to play and then appear to stop, or to start out as a still image and then begin to play, you can split the clip and hold one of the resulting clips. Another approach is to click the Freeze Frame button in the Monitor panel to create a still image from a frame, and then insert that still image at the location of the original frame.

1 Double-click a clip in the Timeline to display it in the Preview window.

2 To hold on a specific frame, rather than the In or Out point of the clip, drag the current-time indicator in the mini-timeline of the Preview window to the frame you want held. Choose Clip > Set Clip Marker > Other Numbered. Then, specify 0 (zero) for Set Numbered Marker, and click OK.

Important: You must set a Clip marker in the clip, not a Timeline marker in the movie.

3 In the Preview window, click the Close button.

4 Select the clip in the Timeline.

5 Choose Clip > Video Options > Frame Hold.

6 In the Frame Hold Options dialog box, select Hold On.

7 Choose the frame you want to hold from the menu: In Point, Out Point, or Marker 0.

8 Specify the following options as desired, and click OK:

Hold Filters Prevents any keyframed effect settings (if any are present) from animating during the duration of the clip. Effect settings use the values at the held frame.

Deinterlace Removes one field from an interlaced video clip and doubles the remaining field, so that interlace artifacts are not apparent in the freeze frame.

Note: If you set the hold frame on an In or Out point, changing the In or Out point doesn't change the freeze frame. On the other hand, if set to hold on Marker 0, moving the marker does change the frame displayed.

For more information, see "Working with source clips" and "Editing clips in their original applications" in Adobe Premiere Elements Help.

Chapter 7: Applying transitions

Transition basics

About transitions

Using *transitions*, you can phase out one clip while phasing in the next or you can stylize the beginning or end of a single clip. A transition can be as subtle as a cross dissolve, or quite emphatic, such as a page turn or spinning pinwheel. While you generally place a transition on a cut to include clips on either side (a *double-sided* transition), you can also apply a transition to just the beginning or end of a clip (a *single-sided* transition).

Page Peel transition between two clips (left) and Cross Dissolve transition at end of clip (right)

For a transition to shift from one clip to the next, the transition must overlap frames from both clips. To achieve the overlap, transitions either use frames previously trimmed from the clips, if any exist (frames just past the In or Out point at the cut), or they repeat the frames on either side of the cut. It's important to remember that when you trim a clip, you don't delete frames. The resulting in and out points simply frame a window over the original clip. A transition uses the trimmed frames to create the transition effect, or, if the clips don't have trimmed frames, the transition repeats frames.

Transition uses trimmed frames to shift to the next scene
A. *First clip with trimmed frames at end* **B.** *Movie containing both clips and transition* **C.** *Second clip with trimmed frames at beginning*

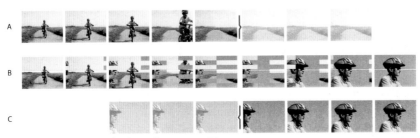

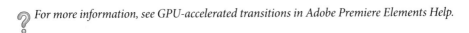

Transition repeats frames for clips without trimmed frames
A. First clip showing last frame repeated **B.** *Movie containing both clips and transition* **C.** *Second clip showing first frame repeated*

For more information, see GPU-accelerated transitions in Adobe Premiere Elements Help.

For more information, see "Where to access transitions" on page 120 and "About effects" on page 131.

Where to access transitions

Available transitions are listed in the Effects And Transitions view of the Media panel and are organized into two main folders, Video Transitions and Audio Transitions. Within these folders, transitions are grouped by type in nested folders. Video transitions have corresponding animated thumbnails that show how they affect clips. (Similarly, effects have image thumbnails.)

If you want to display only the two Transitions folders in Effects And Transitions, click the Transitions button that appears at the top of the panel. You can further customize the panel by creating new folders and grouping transitions in them however you like.

Adobe Premiere Elements includes two audio transitions in the Crossfade category: Constant Power and Constant Gain. Though both provide fades, they differ slightly. Constant Power creates a smoother-sounding fade, while Constant Gain, though mathematically linear, often sounds abrupt.

For more information, see "About audio mixing" on page 183.

Transition appearance in the Sceneline and Timeline

In the Sceneline view of the My Project panel, a transition appears as a rectangle between two clips. In the Timeline view of the My Project panel, a transition appears just above the cut between two clips, or just above the *In* or *Out point* of a single clip.

Transition in Sceneline (above), transition in Timeline (below)

For more information, see "About workspaces and panels" on page 43.

Applying transitions

Applying double- and single-sided transitions

Transitions that gradually replace one clip with another are called *double-sided* transitions. Those that affect only a single clip, as does a fade to black, are called *single-sided*.

Double-sided transitions typically combine the frames at the end of one clip with the frames at the beginning of the clip that follows it. By default, Adobe Premiere Elements will use any frames that follow the out point of the first clip and that precede the in point of the second clip.

If neither clip has these extra frames, Adobe Premiere Elements applies a Center At Cut transition that combines the last frames of the first clip with the first frames of the second. From the beginning of the transition, it repeats, or duplicates, the first frame of the second clip until the cut line. Following the cut line, it repeats the last frame of the first clip to the end of the transition.

You can quickly determine whether a transition is single- or double-sided and whether it has repeated frames, by viewing it in either the Timeline view of the My Project panel, or the Properties panel. A double-sided transition appears as a light rectangle with a dark diagonal line running through it, while a single-sided transition appears as a rectangle split diagonally with one-half dark and one-half light. A transition containing repeated frames has hatch marks running through it.

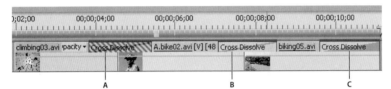

Types of transitions
A. Double-sided transition using repeated frames **B.** *Double-sided transition* **C.** *Single-sided transition*

For more information, see "To create an image mask transition," and "To create a Gradient Wipe transition" in Adobe Premiere Elements Help.

For more information, see "To apply a double-sided transition in the Sceneline" on page 122 and "To apply a double-sided transition in the Timeline" on page 123.

To apply a double-sided transition in the Sceneline

1 Click the Edit Movie button to display the Edit workspace. The Sceneline view of the My Project panel opens by default.

2 Click the Effects and Transitions button ![icon] to open the Effects and Transitions view of the Media panel.

3 In the Media panel, click the Show Transitions button ![icon].

4 Expand the Video Transitions folder, and then expand the folder containing the transition you want to apply.

5 Drag the transition from the Media panel onto a rectangle between two clips in the Sceneline. An icon of the transition fills the rectangle.

6 Double-click the rectangle to preview the transition.

For more information, see "About adjusting effects" on page 139 and "To adjust transition alignment" on page 129.

To apply a double-sided transition in the Timeline

To apply a transition between two clips in the Timeline view of the My Project panel the clips must be on the same track, with no space between them.

If a double-sided transition must use repeated frames (rather than trimmed frames), the transition icon contains additional diagonal lines. The lines span the area where it has used the repeated frames.

1 In the task bar, click the Edit Movie button 🖳 to display the Edit workspace.

2 In the My Project panel, click the Timeline button 🖳 .

3 Click the Effects and Transitions button 🖳 to open the Effects and Transitions view of the Media panel.

4 In the Media panel, expand the Video Transitions folder, and then expand the folder containing the transition you want to apply.

5 Drag the transition from the Media panel to the cut between two clips in the Timeline, and release the mouse button when one of the following alignment icons appears:

Start At Cut ⊨ Aligns the beginning of the transition to the beginning of the second clip.

Center At Cut � Centers the transition over the cut.

End At Cut ⊲| Aligns the end of the transition to the end of the first clip.

💡 *Pressing Ctrl while dragging a transition allows you to select Start At Cut, Center at Cut, or End At Cut by slowly dragging the transition left and right over the cut.*

For more information, see "Aligning double-sided transitions" on page 128 and "About adjusting effects" on page 139.

To apply a single-sided transition in the Sceneline

1 Click the Edit Movie button to display the Edit workspace.

2 In the Media panel, click the Effects And Transitions button.

3 Expand the Video Transitions folder, and then expand the folder containing the transition you want to use.

4 Do one of the following:

- If the clip has no clip adjacent to one side of it, drag the transition to the transition rectangle on that side of the clip.

- If the clip is adjacent to another clip, drag the transition to the desired edge of the clip. In the Alignment pop-up menu in the Properties panel, select either Start at Cut, or End at Cut.

Applying a double-sided transition in the Sceneline

For more information, see "To preview an applied transition" on page 126.

To apply a single-sided transition in the Timeline

When you create a single-sided transition, whatever is below the transition in the Timeline view of the My Project panel appears in the transparent portion of the transition. For example, If you want the clip to transition to black, it must be on track 1 or have no clips beneath it. If the clip is on a track above another clip, the clip on the lower track appears in the transition, so the transition will appear to be double-sided.

1 Click the Edit Movie button to display the Edit workspace.

2 Click the Effects And Transitions button in the Media panel.

3 Expand the Video Transitions folder, and then expand the folder containing the transition you want to use.

4 Do one of the following:

• If the clip has no adjacent clip to one side of it, drag the transition to the edge of the clip.

• If the clip is adjacent to another clip, Ctrl-drag the transition to the edge of the desired clip.

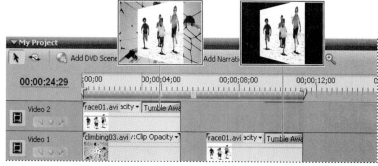

Single-sided transition with clip beneath it (left), and single-sided transition with nothing beneath it (right)

To preview a transition prior to applying it

You can preview an animated thumbnail transition in the Effects And Transitions view of the Media panel without having to apply it to a clip.

1 In the Media panel, click the Effects and Transitions button .

2 Click the Show Transitions button .

3 Click the twirl-down triangle next to Video Transitions, then click the twirl-down triangle next to the type of transition you'd like to preview.

4 Click a thumbnail to set it in motion.

To preview an applied transition

You can preview transitions you've applied from either the Properties panel or the Monitor panel. The Properties panel provides a preview area where you can display thumbnails of the actual clips or the default thumbnails (the letters A and B).

1 In the My Project panel, click the Timeline button 🔲 .

2 Select the transition in the Timeline to display it in the Properties panel.

3 In the Properties panel, click Show Timeline if the Properties timeline is hidden.

4 To display the actual clips in the preview area, select Show Actual Sources. (You may need to lengthen the panel to locate this option.)

5 Do any of the following:

- To preview the transition in the Properties panel, click the Play button ▶ next to the thumbnail. Click the button again to stop the preview.

- To preview the transition in the Monitor panel, move the current-time indicator (in either the Timeline, or the Properties panel) to the left of the transition, and then click the Play button ▶ in the Monitor window.

- To preview a particular frame of the transition in the Monitor panel, drag the current-time indicator (in either the Timeline or the Properties panel) to the desired frame.

If you have a digital camcorder you probably can connect it to both your computer and TV to see real-time previews on the TV monitor. This gives you a better sense of how the transition will look in the finished movie.

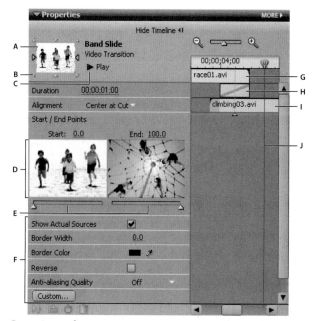

Properties panel
A. Preview button *B.* Transition preview *C.* Play button *D.* Start and End frames *E.* Start and End sliders
F. Options *G.* Clip A (first clip) *H.* Transition *I.* Clip B (second clip) *J.* Current-time indicator

For more information, see "To preview a clip in the Preview window" on page 101.

To specify a default transition

The default transition is used in slide shows you create, files you import from Adobe
Photoshop Elements, and motion backgrounds you create for DVD menus. The default
transitions are Cross Dissolve for video or still images and Constant Power for audio, but
you can change these defaults.

1 In the Media panel, click the Effects and Transitions button ![icon].

2 Select the transition you want to be the default.

3 At the upper right of the panel, click More, and choose Set Selected As Default
Transition. (A blue outline marks the icon of the default transition.)

To make it easy to find transitions that you use frequently, add them to the Favorites folder in Effects And Transitions: Select the transition, and click the Add To Favorites button ☆ .

For more information, see "To adjust transition duration" on page 129.

To replace a transition

You can replace a transition by simply dropping a new transition onto the old one in the Timeline. When you replace a transition, Adobe Premiere Elements maintains the alignment and duration of the original transition; however, it discards the settings of the original transition and instead uses the default settings of the new transition.

1 Click the Edit Movie button in the task bar to display the Edit workspace.

2 In the Media panel, click the Effects and Transitions button 📷 .

3 In Effects And Transitions, open the folder containing the new transition you want to use.

4 Drag the new transition onto the transition in the My Project panel.

For more information, see "Adjusting transition properties," To move a cut and a transition together," and "To adjust the center point of a transition" in Adobe Premiere Elements Help.

Adjusting transitions

Aligning double-sided transitions

Whether clips have trimmed frames determines how you can align a transition between them. The pointer changes to indicate the alignment options as you move it over the cut.

- If both clips contain trimmed frames at the cut, you can center the transition over the cut or align it on either side of the cut so that it either starts or ends at the cut.

- If neither clip contains trimmed frames, the transition automatically centers over the cut and repeats the last frame of the first clip and the first frame of the second clip to fill the transition duration. (Diagonal bars appear on transitions that use repeated frames.)

- If only the first clip contains trimmed frames, the transition automatically snaps to the in point of the next clip. In this scenario, Adobe Premiere Elements uses the first clip's trimmed frames for the transition and does not repeat frames in the second clip.

- If only the second clip contains trimmed frames, then the transition snaps to the out point of the first clip. In this scenario, Adobe Premiere Elements uses the second clip's trimmed frames for the transition and does not repeat frames in the first clip.

For more information, see "To apply a double-sided transition in the Timeline" on page 123 and "To adjust transition alignment" on page 129.

To adjust transition alignment

You can change the alignment of a transition placed between two clips in either the Timeline view of the My Project panel, or the Properties panel. A transition need not be centered or strictly aligned with a cut. You can drag the transition to reposition it over a cut as desired. The Properties panel also contains options to specify alignment.

1 In the My Project panel, click the Timeline button 🖿 .

2 Do any of the following:

- Position the current-time indicator 🚩 over the transition, and then zoom in so that you can clearly see the transition. Drag the transition over the cut to reposition it.

- Select the transition to display it in the Properties panel. (If the timeline in the Properties panel is hidden, click Show Timeline.) In the Properties timeline, position the pointer over the center of the transition until the Slide Transition icon ◄▢► appears; then drag the transition as desired. For finer control, zoom in on the timeline.

- Select the transition to display it in the Properties panel and choose an option from the Alignment pop-up menu.

For more information, see "To apply a double-sided transition in the Sceneline" on page 122 and "To apply a double-sided transition in the Timeline" on page 123.

To adjust transition duration

You can edit a transition's duration by simply dragging the end of the transition in either the Timeline view of the My Project panel, or the Properties panel.

1 In the My Project panel, click the Timeline button 🖿 .

2 Do one of the following:

- Position the pointer over the end of the transition until the Trim-In icon ◄╂ or the Trim-Out icon ╂► appears.

- Select the transition to display it in the Properties panel. (If the timeline in the Properties panel is hidden, click Show Timeline.) In the Properties timeline, position the pointer over the transition until the Trim-In icon or the Trim-Out icon appears; then drag.

- Select the transition to display it in the Properties panel. In the Properties panel, drag the Duration value, or select it and type a new value.

Note: Lengthening a transition's duration requires that one or both clips have enough trimmed frames to accommodate a longer transition.

Chapter 8: Applying effects

Effects basics

About effects

After you've assembled a movie (arranging, deleting, and trimming clips), you can add polish to it by applying effects to clips. For example, an effect can alter the exposure or color of footage, manipulate sound, distort images, or add artistic effects. You can also use effects to rotate and animate a clip or adjust its size and position within the frame. Adobe Premiere Elements also includes several preset effects that you can use to quickly alter your footage.

To apply an effect, you drag it from the Media panel to a clip in the My Project panel or Monitor panel. The properties of the effect are then added to the Properties panel for that media file. Most effects have adjustable properties; however, some effects, such as Black & White, do not. If you want to adjust an effect's properties, use either the Timeline view of the My Project panel, or the Properties panel.

 For more information, see "Effects reference" in Adobe Premiere Elements Help.

For more information, see "To apply and preview a video effect" on page 134 and "About transitions" on page 119.

Understanding standard and fixed effects

You can apply any number or combination of effects from the Media panel to each media file in the My Project panel. These effects add special characteristics to your image or audio, or they correct a problem, such as low light levels in video clips or hiss in audio clips.

Adobe Premiere Elements automatically applies *fixed effects* (Image Control, Motion, Opacity, and Volume) to every clip in the My Project panel. Fixed effects can't be removed or reordered, and they don't affect a clip until you change the effect properties. The Image Control effect lets you control the brightness, contrast, hue, and saturation of video clips. The Motion effect lets you reposition, scale, anchor, and rotate video clips, and remove flicker from them. The Opacity effect lets you create fades and dissolves for special effects or transitions. The Volume effect lets you control the volume of audio clips. Effects that aren't fixed are called *standard effects*.

For more information, see "Adding effects to Adobe Premiere Elements," and "GPU-accelerated effects" in Adobe Premiere Elements Help.

For more information, see "To apply and preview a video effect" on page 134 and "About adjusting effects" on page 139.

Finding and organizing effects

Where to access effects

Available effects are listed in the Effects And Transitions view 🔲 of the Media panel. Setting aside the folders for transitions, presets, and favorites, the effects are organized into two main folders: Video Effects and Audio Effects. Preconfigured effects (effect presets) are stored in the Presets folder, and effect presets you create are stored in the My Presets folder. You can also add a Favorites folder to store your favorite or most frequently used effects. You can control which folders appear by clicking the buttons that appear at the top of the panel.

Within each folder, effects are grouped by type in nested folders. For example, the Blur And Sharpen folder contains effects that alter the clarity or focus of an image, such as Fast Blur and Sharpen. Video transitions have animated thumbnail previews that show how they affect clips. Select a transition to set its thumbnail in motion.

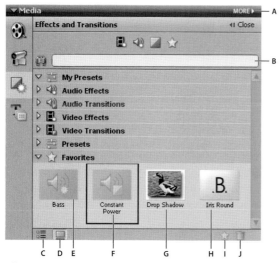

Effects And Transitions view of the Media panel
A. *More menu* **B.** *Search text box* **C.** *List View button* **D.** *Thumbnail View button* **E.** *Audio effect* **F.** *Audio transition* **G.** *Video effect* **H.** *Video transition* **I.** *Favorites button* **J.** *Delete Custom Items button*

For more information, see "To organize effects and transitions," and "To rename or delete a custom folder" in Adobe Premiere Elements Help.

For more information, see "To apply and preview a video effect" on page 134.

To find an effect

❖ Click the Effects And Transitions button ![icon] in the Media panel, and do one of the following:

• In the text box, type the name of the effect that you are looking for. The list displays all effects with names that match the letters and spaces you type. (Clear the text box to see all of the effect folders.)

• Click a folder to expand it and view its contents. To change the display of the contents, click the List View ![icon] button or Thumbnail View ![icon] button.

Click the buttons across the top of the panel to display a subset of the effect folders. For example, click this button ![icon] to display only the My Presets, Video Effects, and Presets folders. Click in the text box to display all of the folders.

Applying and removing effects

About applying effects

By default, when you apply an effect to a clip, the effect is active for the duration of the clip. After you apply an effect, you can adjust its properties in the Properties panel. You can make an effect start and stop at specific times or adjust the values of the effect over time by using *keyframes*. (For information, see "About keyframes" on page 143.)

You can apply multiple effects to a clip, and you can even apply the same effect numerous times to the same clip with different settings. Keep in mind, however, that the more effects you add, the more time it takes for Adobe Premiere Elements to render the final movie. You can also easily delete effects that you decide are not suitable for your project.

Note: Most audio effects can be applied to both clips and tracks. Each audio effect includes a bypass option that lets you turn the effect on or off as specified by the keyframes that you set.

To apply and preview a video effect

1 Click the Edit Movie button to open the Edit workspace. The Properties panel, and the Sceneline view of the My Project panel open by default.

2 Click the Effects and Transitions button 🔧 in the Media panel. This opens the Effects and Transitions view of the Media panel.

3 In Effects And Transitions, locate the effect in the Video Effects folder, or type the effect name in the text box.

4 Select a clip in the Sceneline. The clip appears in the Monitor.

5 Drag a video effect to the Monitor or to the Properties panel. This applies the effect to the clip.

6 Click the Play button ▶ in the Monitor panel to preview the clip with the effect applied.

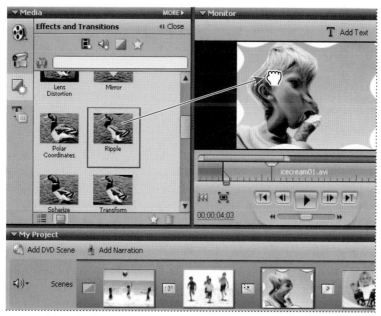

Dragging the Ripple effect to a clip

For more information, see "To temporarily disable an effect in a video clip" in Adobe Premiere Elements Help.

For more information, see "To apply an effect preset" on page 139 and "About adjusting effects" on page 139.

To apply an audio effect

1 In the task bar, click the Edit Movie button to open the Edit workspace. The Properties panel, and the Sceneline view of the My Project panel open by default.

2 In the My Project panel, click the Timeline button .

3 Click the Effects and Transitions button in the Media panel. This opens the Effects and Transitions view of the Media panel.

4 In Effects And Transitions, locate the effect in the Audio Effects folder, or type the effect name in the box.

5 Select a clip in the Timeline. The clip appears in the Monitor.

6 Drag an audio effect to the clip's sound track in the Timeline, the Monitor, or the Properties panel. This applies the effect to the clip.

For more information, see "To temporarily disable an effect in an audio clip" in Adobe Premiere Elements Help.

To preview an audio effect

You can preview the sound track of any clip in the My Project panel to hear the results of audio effects and transitions applied to it.

❖ Click the Play Only Audio For This Clip button ▶♪ in the lower left of the Properties panel. To play audio as a continuous loop, click the Looping Audio Playback button 📤 before you click Play Audio.

Note: Audio playback controls are available only if the selected clip contains audio.

Copying and pasting effects

You can copy and paste one or more effects from one clip (source clip) to another (target clip) by using the Properties panel. You can also copy all effect values (including keyframes for effects) from one clip to another by using the Paste Attributes command in the Timeline. Similarly, you can copy effects from one project into another. You can copy and paste effects in either the Sceneline view or the Timeline view of the My Project panel.

If the effect includes keyframes, the keyframes appear at comparable positions in the target clip, starting at the beginning of the clip. If the target clip is shorter than the source clip, keyframes are pasted beyond the target clip's Out point. To view these keyframes, move the clip's Out point to a time later than the keyframe's placement or deselect the Pin To Clip option. (In the Properties panel, click the More button and deselect Pin To Clip.)

To copy and paste specific effects

1 In the My Project panel, click the Timeline button 🖳 .

2 In the Timeline, select the clip that contains the effect you want to copy.

3 In the Properties panel, select the effects you want to copy. (Shift-click or Ctrl-click to select multiple effects.)

4 Choose Edit > Copy.

5 In the Timeline, select the clip you want to receive the copied effects.

6 Click the Properties panel to make it active.

7 Choose Edit > Paste.

To copy and paste all effects

1 In the My Project panel, click the Timeline button 📑 .

2 In the Timeline, select the clip that contains the effects you want to copy.

3 Choose Edit > Copy. This copies all the attributes of the clip.

4 In the Timeline, select the clip you want to receive the effects.

5 Choose Edit > Paste Attributes. This pastes all the attributes of the first clip to the second.

To remove an effect

1 In the My Project panel, click the Timeline button 📑 .

2 In the Timeline, select the clip containing the effect that you want to delete, and do one of the following:

• To delete an effect at any time, select the effect that you want to delete in the Properties panel, and press Delete or Backspace. Alternatively, click the More button, and choose Delete Selected Effect or Delete All Effects From Clip.

• To immediately delete an effect that you just applied, choose Edit > Undo. (You can choose an unlimited number of undos.) Alternatively, use the History panel. Choose Window > History, select the last Apply Filter action in the list, and click the Delete Redoable Actions button 🗑 . You can select any previous Apply Filter action as well, but note that if you performed other actions after the Apply Filter action, deleting the Apply Filter action also deletes the actions below it.

Note: *You cannot remove the fixed effects: Image Control, Motion, Opacity, and Volume. However, you can reset them.*

For more information, see "To reset an effect to its default properties" on page 141.

Working with effect presets

About effect presets

Adobe Premiere Elements includes several effect presets, which are common, precon-figured effects that you can apply to clips. For instance, the Tint Blue preset adds a light blue tint to an entire image. Typically, presets provide good results without having to adjust their properties. Once you apply a preset, you can change its properties to your liking. You can also create your own presets.

The effect presets included with Adobe Premiere Elements are stored in the Presets folder in the Effects And Transitions view of the Media panel. Presets are grouped in the following categories:

Bevel Edges Create thick or thin edges that resemble picture frames.

Blurs Create blurs of varying degrees at the In or Out points of a clip.

Color Effects Create tints of varying color and intensity.

Drop Shadows Create either static or animated shadows. Shadow presets have suffixes that indicate the direction that the shadow is cast or the direction that it moves. For example, LL indicates that the shadow is cast to the lower left. For moving shadows, the appendix is hyphenated, so LR-LL indicates that the shadow moves from the lower right to the lower left. To ensure that shadows are visible, apply shadows to images that are smaller than the project's frame size and make sure that the background image is not black.

Horizontal/Vertical Image Pans Create animations in which the entire image moves left and right or up and down as the video plays. For example, an L-R horizontal pan moves the image from left to right.

Horizontal/Vertical Image Zooms Create animated zoom effects.

Mosaics, Solarizes, and Twirls Create animated effects that either decreases in intensity from the beginning of the clip, or increases in intensity as the clip ends.

PiPs Create Picture-in-Picture effects by scaling the target clip so that you can superimpose it onto a full-sized clip. You can also apply this effect to several clips in order to create a montage.

Note: For descriptions of the effects used in the presets, search for the effect name in Adobe Premiere Elements Help.

For more information, see "About effects" on page 131.

To apply an effect preset

If you apply a preset to a clip, and the preset contains properties for an effect that is already applied to the clip, Adobe Premiere Elements modifies the clip using the following rules:

• If the effect preset contains a fixed effect (Image Control, Motion, Opacity, or Volume), applying the preset replaces the existing effect properties.

• If the effect preset contains a standard (non-fixed) effect, the effect is added to the bottom of the list of effects.

1 Click the Edit Movie button to open the Edit workspace.

2 In the Media panel, click the Effects and Transitions button 🔧 .

3 Expand the Presets folder, and drag an effect preset into the Properties panel.

4 To preview the effect, click the Play button ▶ in the Monitor.

⚲ *For more information, see "To create an effect preset" in Adobe Premiere Elements Help.*

For more information, see "About adjusting effects" on page 139.

Adjusting effects

About adjusting effects

To adjust effect properties, you use the Properties panel. The Properties panel includes a time ruler, a current-time indicator, zoom controls, controls for playing and looping audio clips, and a keyframe navigator. Unlike the time ruler in the Timeline view of the My Project panel, the time ruler in the Properties panel measures only a specific clip or transition. Click Show Keyframes to view the time ruler and the keyframe area, where you can adjust how an effect changes over time.

In the Properties panel, you can view the entire length of a clip to which you apply an effect. Expand an effect to display the controls that you use to change its properties. Controls can include underlined values, sliders, effect point icons, angle controls, menus, color swatches, the Eyedropper tool, and graphs.

> *To quickly optimize your workspace for applying and adjusting effects, choose Window >*
> *Restore Workspace > Edit.*

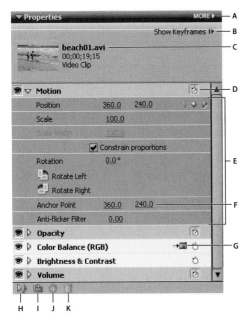

Properties panel
A. *More menu* **B.** *Show/Hide Keyframes button* **C.** *Clip name* **D.** *Toggle Animation button (also Keyframe summary icon)* **E.** *Effect properties* **F.** *Property values* **G.** *Setup button* **H.** *Play Audio button* **I.** *Loop Audio button* **J.** *Reset button* **K.** *Delete button*

For more information, see "About keyframes" on page 143 and "To adjust effect properties" on page 140.

To adjust effect properties

You can adjust Volume and Opacity effects in the Timeline view of the My Project panel. You can also adjust these, and the properties for all other effects, in the Properties panel, using either the Sceneline view or the Timeline view of the My Project panel.

1 In the My Project panel, click the Timeline button 🖥 .

2 In the Timeline, select the clip that contains the effect you want to adjust.

3 In the Properties panel, expand the effect and do any of the following:

- Drag the underlined value left or right.

- Click the underlined value, enter a new value, and press Enter.

- Drag inside the angle control area. Once you've clicked inside the angle control, you can drag outside of it to quickly change the values.

- Expand the property by clicking the triangle next to the property name (if available), and then drag the slider or angle control (depending on the property).

4 Preview your changes in the Monitor panel.

If you have a DV camcorder, you may be able to preview effects on a TV monitor. Connect the computer to your DV camcorder's FireWire˜ jack and connect the camcorder's audio and video outputs to the TV. Previewing on a TV monitor is especially helpful for changes to color.

For more information, see "Adjusting volume levels" on page 183.

To reset an effect to its default properties

When you reset an effect, all properties that don't contain keyframes are reset to their default values. If a property contains keyframes, that property is reset to the default at the current time only. Keyframes that occur at the current time are reset to the default value. If no keyframes occur at the current time, new keyframes are created using the default values.

1 In the My Project panel, click the Timeline button .

2 In the Timeline, select the clip that contains the effect you want to reset.

3 In the Properties panel, click the effect name.

4 Click the Reset button .

The Reset button doesn't deactivate keyframing for the property. If you accidently click Reset, restore your work by choosing Edit > Undo.

For more information, see "Adjusting effects," "Superimposing and transparency," and "Selecting colors for effects and mattes" in Adobe Premiere Elements Help.

Chapter 9: Animating effects

Effect animation basics

About keyframes

Keyframes are those frames of video at which specific values are set for properties of an effect. A property is seen to change in time as its values change from one keyframe to the next. Setting values in keyframes, then, is the fundamental way to animate an effect. You can animate effects either with presets which have predefined keyframe values, or with keyframes you create, to which you apply custom values. Presets provide a quick, easy way to animate effects, whereas custom keyframes let you create more precise and complex animations.

With each keyframe, you specify a value for an effect property at a specific point in time. Adobe Premiere Elements *interpolates* the values between keyframes, creating a transition from one keyframe to the next. For example, to create a blur effect that changes over time, you could set three keyframes—the first with no blur, the second with blur, and the third with no blur. Through *interpolation,* the blur gradually increases between the first and second keyframes and then gradually decreases between the second and third keyframes.

Animating with keyframes involves three basic steps:

1 Apply an effect or preset to a clip. (See "To apply and preview a video effect" on page 134.)

2 Add multiple keyframes for that effect.

3 Specify keyframe values for effect properties.

Note: Some effects cannot be animated with keyframes. For details, see the documentation for individual effects.

Highlighted frames indicate where Twirl effect keyframes have been added
A. Original video B. Video with animated Twirl effect, interpolated for in-between frames

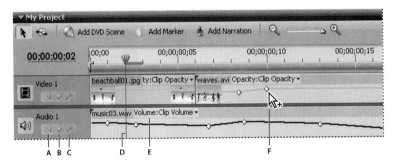

Keyframe controls in the Timeline view of the My Project panel
A. Previous Keyframe button B. Add Keyframe button C. Next Keyframe button D. Current-time indicator
E. Effect properties menu F. Add Keyframe pointer

For more information, see "About effects" on page 131 and "Where to access effects" on page 132.

Guidelines for working with keyframes

You can view and edit keyframes in either the Timeline view of the My Project panel, or the Properties panel. In general, the Timeline is appropriate for quickly viewing and adjusting keyframes for a single effect. The Properties panel is more appropriate for detailed changes to multiple keyframe values. Also use the Properties panel to edit keyframes while using the Sceneline view of the My Project panel.

Use these guidelines to help you choose the panel appropriate for a task.

- The Timeline is best for editing the keyframes of effects that have a single, one-dimensional value, such as Opacity or Volume.

- The Properties panel is best for editing the keyframes of effects that have multiple or two-dimensional values, such as Motion or Perspective.

- The Properties panel displays all effect properties, keyframes, and interpolation methods at once, but only for a single selected clip. The Timeline can display the keyframes for multiple clips at once, but it can display only one property per clip.

If you want to animate a clip's Motion effect, you can work directly in the Monitor panel, while adding keyframes in the Timeline or the Properties panel.

Displaying, adding, and removing keyframes

To display keyframes in the Properties panel

When you work in the Properties panel, you can show or hide the keyframe area to make it easier for you to work. To maximize keyframing space, you can undock the Properties panel and drag it into its own window. You can also set the length of the time ruler in the keyframes area so that it matches a clip's *In* and *Out points*, or you can extend the ruler to match all clips in the My Project panel. Extending the time ruler is helpful if you want to see the context in which you're applying an effect.

- To show the keyframe area, click the Show Keyframes button in the Properties panel. The button changes to the Hide Keyframes button. Click the button again to hide the keyframe area.

- To match the time ruler to a clip's In and Out points, click the More button in the Properties panel, and select Pin To Clip from the menu. (This option is selected by default.) Deselect this option to extend the time ruler to match all clips in the My Project panel.

- To expand or contract the time ruler, drag the time ruler slider to left or right.

You can view any keyframe in the keyframe area of the Properties panel. Any effect that contains animated properties displays *a Summary Keyframe* 🔘 when the effect is collapsed. Summary keyframes appear in the keyframe area and correspond to all the individual property keyframes contained in the effect. You can't manipulate summary keyframes; they appear for reference only.

1 Select a clip in the My Project panel to display it in the Properties panel.

2 If the keyframe area is hidden, click Show Keyframes. You might have to enlarge the Properties panel to see the keyframe area.

To add keyframes in the Properties panel

In the Properties panel, Adobe Premiere Elements creates keyframes automatically when you move the current-time indicator and change property values, if the Toggle Animation button is selected. You can also create keyframes manually by using the Add/Remove Keyframe button. You must create at least two keyframes with different values to vary an effect over time.

Note: If a keyframe is created before the first or after the last existing keyframe for a property, the new keyframe acquires the same value as that existing keyframe. If it falls between keyframes, however, the new keyframe acquires a value interpolated between the values of the previous and next keyframes.

1 In the My Project panel, select the clip that contains the effect you want to animate.

2 In the Properties panel, expand the effect. If the keyframe area is hidden, click Show Keyframes. You might have to enlarge the Properties panel to see the keyframe area.

3 Click the Toggle Animation button ⏱ to activate keyframes for the effect properties. This will set the first keyframe for each of the properties of the effect chosen.

4 Move the current-time indicator to where you want to add a keyframe.

5 Do one of the following:

- Click the Add/Remove Keyframe button ◆ .

- Adjust the value for the effect property.

6 Repeat steps 4 and 5 as needed.

 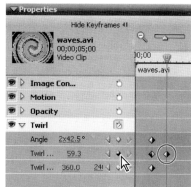

A	B

Adding keyframes in properties panel
A. Click Toggle Animation button to activate keyframes for all properties of an effect. ***B.*** *To right of property settings, Add/Remove Keyframe button becomes available for adding or removing keyframes for each property individually.*

For information about displaying and adding keyframes in the Timeline, see, Adobe Premiere Elements Help.

To remove a keyframe

❖ Do one of the following:

- Select the clip in the My Project panel to display it in the Properties panel. (If the keyframe area is hidden, click Show Keyframes. You might have to enlarge the Properties panel to see the keyframe area.) Select one or more keyframes and press Delete. Alternatively, drag the current-time indicator in the Properties panel to the keyframe, and click the Add/Remove Keyframe button.

- From the effect properties menu right above the clip in the Timeline view of the My Project panel, choose the property that contains the keyframe. Select the keyframe and press Delete. Alternatively, select the keyframe and click the Add/Remove Keyframe button , which is below the track name in the Timeline.

For more information about removing or copying keyframes, see Adobe Premiere Elements Help.

Adjusting keyframes

Specifying keyframe values

To animate an effect, you specify different property values across keyframes. In the Timeline view of the My Project panel, you can change the values by dragging keyframe icons up or down. This method works best for simple Opacity and Volume adjustments. In the Properties panel, you can make more detailed changes to multiple properties.

To specify keyframe values in the Properties panel

In the Properties panel, you drag or enter property values to adjust keyframes. To change the value of an existing keyframe, you must position the current-time indicator at the keyframe; changing a property value where no keyframe exists creates a new keyframe if the Toggle Animation button ⏱ is depressed.

1 Expand the effect property that contains keyframes you want to specify values for.

2 Click the Previous Keyframe button ◀ or the Next Keyframe button ▶ to select the keyframe.

• Drag or enter the property value. (For information about a particular effect property, search for the effect name in Adobe Premiere Elements Help.)

To specify keyframe values in the Timeline

In the Timeline view of the My Project panel, you increase or decrease values by vertically dragging individual keyframes or entire keyframe graphs. This method works best for simple Opacity and Volume adjustments. For more detailed changes, use the Properties panel.

As you drag a keyframe or graph, a tool tip displays its location and value. Note that the effect property determines the units and values that appear.

1 From the effect properties menu right above the clip, choose the property you want to specify values for. (You may need to zoom in to see the menu.)

2 With the Selection tool ➤ , do any of the following:

• To change an individual keyframe, drag it. (The pointer changes to the keyframe-editing icon ▸ .)

- To change multiple or nonadjacent keyframes, Shift-click them, and then drag. (The pointer changes to the keyframe-editing icon ↳◊ .)

- To change the keyframe graph, drag it. (The pointer changes to the graph-editing icon ↳‡.)

For more information, see "Adjusting keyframes," "Controlling change between keyframes," and "Animating a clip's position" in Adobe Premiere Elements Help.

Chapter 10: Creating titles

Creating and trimming titles

About creating titles

You can design custom titles and graphics with Adobe Premiere Elements. Titles serve many purposes, from identifying people and places onscreen to providing movie-style credits at the beginning and end. You can create titles using any font installed on your computer, and other graphic objects using the shape creation tools.

You can have your text run horizontally or vertically. You can stretch it or shrink it, or give it a color or shadow. You can have it hold still on the screen, crawl across it horizontally, roll vertically, or move across a path you define.

You can either create your titles from scratch by using the text and shape tools or use one of the included templates, preset text styles, or images to quickly create an attractive title.

Though the titling tools are powerful, they are easy to use. You can begin simply by clicking the Add Text button and typing into the Monitor panel.

You can edit titles like other clips in the Monitor panel and the Timeline view of the My Project panel, or trim them in the Preview window.

Titles are embedded into the project file; they are not saved as independent files. However, you can export a title to an Adobe Premiere Elements title file, with the prtl file extension, for use in another Adobe Premiere Elements project. Select File > Export > Title.

Adding text
A. Monitor panel B. Tools C. Properties panel

About superimposing titles

Before creating a title, select a place for it. You can superimpose a title on a video clip, or place it in an empty area of the My Project panel with no underlying video. If you choose the latter, you can still superimpose it later by using a simple drag-and-drop procedure.

When you create a title in an empty area, Adobe Premiere Elements places it in the Video 1 track of the Timeline and into an empty target area in the Sceneline.

Note: *If you drag a clip onto a title in the Sceneline, or place one on a track above the title in the Timeline, the clip will obscure the title, usually making the title disappear from the Monitor panel. To make the title visible again, click the Timeline button in the My Project panel and drag the title to a video track higher than the track holding the clip.*

To create a new still title

This procedure shows you how to create a still, non-moving title. To create titles that scroll or crawl across the screen, see "To create a rolling or crawling title" on page 175.

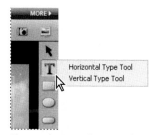

Choosing horizontal or vertical type for titles

1 In the My Project panel, click the Sceneline button ▮▯▮ .

2 Do one of the following:

• To superimpose the new title on a video clip, select the clip in the Sceneline.

• To add a title without underlying video, select an empty target area in the Sceneline.

3 Do one of the following:

• In the Monitor panel, click the Add Text button T .

• Choose Title > New Title > Default Still.

• Choose File > New > Title.

• In the Media panel, click the New Item button ▢ and choose Title.

Adobe Premiere Elements places default text in the Monitor panel and puts it in title-editing mode.

4 Do either of the following:

• To add horizontal type, double-click the default text, and type to replace it.

• To add vertical type, click and hold the Type Tool button T . Then choose Vertical Type Tool. Click anywhere in the Monitor panel, and type your title.

5 In the Monitor panel, click the Selection Tool ➤ .

Adobe Premiere Elements saves the title and adds it to the Media panel and the My Project panel.

Note: *While editing a title, you can add an additional title only by clicking the Add Text button.*

For more information, see "About templates" on page 155 and "About rolling and crawling titles" on page 174.

To trim all instances of a title

To trim all instances of a title throughout a movie, use the Media panel.

1 In the Media panel, click the Available Media button ⬤ .

2 Double-click the title in the Media panel.

Adobe Premiere Elements opens the title in the Preview window.

3 In the Preview window, do one of the following:

- Drag either the Set In handle ▮ or the Set Out handle ▮ to trim the title.

- Drag the current-time indicator to the desired location and click either the Set In button ▮ or the Set Out button ▮ to establish a new in point or out point.

4 In the Preview window, click the Close button ✖ .

Adobe Premiere Elements saves the trimmed title in the Media panel.

For more information, see "To trim an individual title instance" on page 154.

To trim an individual title instance

To trim an individual instance of a title, select it in the My Project panel. This affects the length of the instance of the title in the My Project panel, not the length of the original clip in the Media panel.

1 In the My Project panel, click either the Sceneline button ▮▮▮ or the Timeline button ▦ .

2 Do one of the following:

- If you're using the Sceneline, in the Monitor panel, right-click, choose Select, and choose the name of the title to be trimmed. A representation of the title appears in the Monitor panel's mini-timeline as a lavender bar containing the title filename .

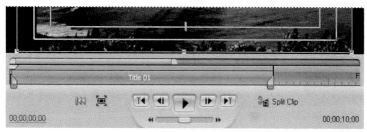

A title in the Monitor panel's mini-timeline

- If you're using the Timeline, locate the title to be trimmed in one of the video tracks. You might need to drag the video track scroll bar in the My Project panel to expose the title.

3 Do one of the following:

- If using the Sceneline, in the Monitor panel, drag either the Set In handle ▮ or the Set Out handle ▮ of the title representation to trim the title.

- If using the Timeline, hover the cursor over either end of the title until it changes to the ripple trim cursor ◆. Then drag the end of the title to trim it and close any gap created by the trim. To trim without closing the gap, Ctrl-drag the clip end instead.

For more information, see "To trim all instances of a title" on page 154.

Creating titles from templates

About templates

The title templates included with Adobe Premiere Elements provide several themes and preset layouts that make it quick and easy to design a title. Some templates include graphic images that may be pertinent to your movie's subject matter, such as new baby or vacation themes. Others include placeholder text that you can replace to create credits for your movie. Some templates have transparent backgrounds, depicted by black backgrounds, allowing you to see your video beneath the title; others are completely opaque.

You can easily change every text or graphic object in the template by selecting the object and either deleting it or overwriting it. You can also add additional objects to the title. After you make modifications, your unique version of the title is saved with your project without affecting the template on which it's based.

Note: When you apply a new template, the template content replaces any content currently in the Monitor panel.

For more information, see "About adding images" on page 165.

To create a new title from a template

1 In the Media panel, click the Title Templates button 🔲.

2 Browse to a template by clicking the twirl-down triangles next to folder icons.

3 Do one of the following:

• Click the Sceneline button 🔲 in the My Project panel, drag a template from Title Templates onto one of the target areas in the Sceneline. If there is a clip in the target area, it will move to the right to make room for the new title.

• Click the Sceneline button 🔲 in the My Project panel, select a target area of the Sceneline, and drag a template from Title Templates onto the Monitor panel. If there is a clip in the target area, the new title will be superimposed on it.

• Click the Timeline button 🔲 in the My Project panel, and drag a template onto any location of a video track in the Timeline.

• Click the Timeline button 🔲 in the My Project panel, drag the current-time indicator to the place where you want the title, and drag the template onto the Monitor panel.

4 Modify the title as needed.

Designing titles for TV

Previewing titles on a TV monitor

If your intended audience will view your finished program on a TV, preview the program on a TV monitor as you work. Elements that appear satisfactory on a computer screen may be unacceptable when viewed on a TV because computer monitors and TV monitors display images differently. The outer edges of the image may be cropped, colors may bleed, and horizontal details may appear to flicker. However, once you are aware of a problem, it's easy to take steps to correct it.

Safe Title and Safe Action margins

The Safe Title and Safe Action margins in the Monitor panel designate the title's visible safe zones. These margins are displayed by default when the Monitor is in title-editing mode.

Safe zones are useful when editing for broadcast and videotape. Most consumer TV sets use a process called *overscan*, which cuts off a portion of the outer edges of the picture, allowing the center of the picture to be enlarged. The amount of overscan is not consistent across TVs, so to ensure that titles and important actions fit within the area that most TVs display, keep text within the safe title margins and all other important elements within the safe action margins.

Note: *If you are creating content for the Web or a CD, the safe title and safe action margins do not apply to your project because the entire image is displayed in these mediums.*

Safe title and safe action margins
A. Safe title margin B. Safe action margin

To display or hide safe margins

❖ While adding text or editing a title, do one of the following:

- In the Monitor panel, click the More button and choose Safe Title Margin, Safe Action Margin, or both.

- Choose Title > View > Safe Title Margin, Safe Action Margin, or both.

- Right-click in the Monitor panel and choose View > Safe Title Margin, Safe Action Margin, or both.

A margin is displayed if a check mark appears next to its menu item.

To change the sizes of the safe margins

You can adjust the sizes of the Title Safe area, the Action Safe area, or both (for example, to customize them for displays with less overscan).

1 Select Edit > Project Settings > General.

This opens the Project Settings dialog box.

2 In the Video pane, type new horizontal or vertical percentage values for Title Safe Area, Action Safe Area, or both. Click OK.

Editing and formatting text

To select and edit title text

1 Using the Selection tool in the Monitor panel, double-click the word you want to edit or the spot where you want to begin a selection. The tool changes to the Type tool. If a word was clicked, it becomes highlighted.

2 Do one of the following:

- To move the insertion point, click between characters or use the left arrow and right arrow keys.

- To select a single character or group of contiguous characters, drag from the blinking insertion point cursor to highlight the characters.

You can format selected text using controls in the Properties panel or using menu commands. To format an entire text or graphic object, click the object to select it and then modify its attributes.

For more information, see "About formatting text" on page 159.

To wrap text automatically

1 If the Monitor panel is not already in title-editing mode, click the Add Text button T or double-click an existing title in the Monitor panel.

2 Do one of the following:

- Choose Title > Word Wrap.

- Right-click in the Monitor panel and choose Word Wrap.

3 Click in the Monitor panel and type your title.

Adobe Premiere Elements automatically wraps the words, starting a new line of text whenever the cursor reaches the safe-title margin.

About formatting text

Some object properties—such as fill color, shadow, and so on—are common to all objects you create, while other properties are unique to text objects. You can find text controls such as typeface, typeface style, and type alignment, in the Properties panel, the Title menu, and the pop-up menu that appears when you right-click a box in the Monitor panel. Other options are available in the Color Properties dialog box and Title menu.

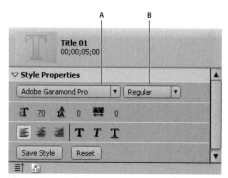

Font options in the Properties panel
A. *Typeface* **B.** *Typeface style*

Note: *You can quickly apply a favorite set of attributes (color, shadow, and so on) to any object by using the Styles section of the Properties panel. (See "About styles" on page 162.)*

To specify a typeface

❖ Select the text and do one of the following:

- In the Properties panel, choose a typeface from the typeface menu in the Properties panel.
- Choose Title > Font, and choose a typeface from the menu.

To specify a typeface style

Many typefaces include built-in variations on the typeface, such as bold, italic, and narrow fonts. The specific variations depend on the typeface.

❖ Select the text and choose a typeface style from the typeface style menu (next to the typeface menu in the Properties panel).

To make text bold, italic, or underlined

If a typeface includes bold, italic, or underlined styles, you can add those options using buttons in the Properties panel. If the typeface doesn't include bold or italic versions, then their buttons appear dimmed. You can underline any font.

❖ Select text and click any of the following in the Properties panel:

- **T** makes the selected text bold
- *T* makes the selected text italic
- T̲ makes the selected text underlined

Note: *The Bold button is also available if the typeface style menu includes a variation called "heavy."*

To change the typeface size

❖ Select the text and do one of the following:

- In the Properties panel, change the value next to the typeface size icon **T**.
- Choose Title > Size and choose a typeface size.

To set the spacing between text characters

The spacing between pairs of characters is called *kerning*. At times, you may want to adjust the kerning to make the text more pleasing to the eye or to make a line of text take up more or less space.

1 Do one of the following:

- To adjust the space between a range of characters, select the range of text, or the entire text object.

- To adjust the space between a pair of characters, set the insertion point (the blinking cursor) between the characters.

2 Change the value next to the Kerning icon in the Properties panel.

To set the spacing between lines of text

The spacing between lines of text is called *leading*. At times, you may want to adjust the leading to make a block of text more pleasing to the eye, or to make it take up more or less space on the screen.

1 Do one of the following:

- To adjust the space between all lines of text, select the text object.

- To adjust the space between two lines, set the insertion point anywhere in the second line.

2 Change the value next to the Leading icon in the Properties panel.

To change text orientation

1 Select a text object.

2 Choose Title > Orientation and select either Horizontal or Vertical.

To change paragraph text alignment

1 Select a paragraph text object.

2 In the Properties panel, click the triangle next to Style Properties, if necessary to expand it. Do one of the following:

- To align text with the left side of the box, click Left Align Text .

- To center the text in the box, click Center Text .

- To align text on the right side in the box, click Right Align Text ▤ .

To reflow paragraph text

1 Select a paragraph text object.

2 Drag any handle of the text's bounding box to resize the box.

Applying styles to text and graphics

About styles

Adobe Premiere Elements includes a number of styles for use in titling. Each of these contains predetermined values for such attributes as typeface, stroke, color, and drop shadow that convey a pleasing design to titling elements. Styles can be applied to text, graphics, or both.

Adobe Premiere Elements applies a default style to every graphic and block of text you create. You can change this style by selecting one of the provided styles or by modifying it into a style of your own.

You can save a combination of color properties and font characteristics as a *style* that you can then apply to any text or shape element in your title. You can save any number of styles. Thumbnails of the styles appear in the Styles section ▜ in the Properties panel when the Monitor panel is in title-editing mode. Your custom styles appear among those provided so you can quickly apply your custom styles across projects.

Right-click a style to quickly access options from a context menu.

To create a style and display its swatch or name

1 Select an object that has the properties you want to save as a style.

2 In Style Properties in the Properties panel, click Save Style.

3 Type a name for the style and click OK. Depending upon the display option you select, either a swatch displaying the new style or the new style name appears in Title Styles ${T_T}$.

Note: Styles are always represented by a typeface, even if the object on which you based the style is a shape object.

To apply a style to an object

1 Select the object to which you want to apply the style.

2 In the Styles section ${T_T}$ of the Properties panel, click the style swatch that you want to apply.

To delete, duplicate, rename, or set a style

❖ In the Styles section ${T_T}$ of the Properties panel, do any of the following:

• To delete a style, right-click the style, and then choose Delete Style.

Note: You can restore the preset library by clicking the Reset button in the Style Properties section of the Properties panel.

• To duplicate a style, right-click the style, and then choose Duplicate Style. A duplicate of the selected style appears in Styles.

• To rename a style, right-click the style, and then choose Rename Style. Type a new name in the Rename Style dialog box, and click OK. In Roman languages, names containing more than 32 characters are truncated.

• To set a default style, right-click the style, and then choose Set Style As Default. The default style's thumbnail becomes the first thumbnail in Styles and is the style automatically applied when you create a new title.

Note: The most recent style you select remains selected until you choose a new style or create a new title. When you create a new title, the default style is selected.

Adding shapes and images to titles

Creating shapes

You can also use the drawing tools in the Monitor panel to create a variety of shapes, such as rectangles, ellipses, and lines.

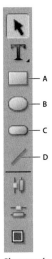

Shape tools
A. Rectangle B. Ellipse C. Rounded Rectangle D. Line

To create shapes

1 Select a shape tool.

2 Do any of the following:

- Shift-drag to constrain the shape's aspect ratio.

- Alt-drag to draw from the center of the shape.

- Shift+Alt-drag to constrain the aspect ratio and draw from the center.

- Drag diagonally across the corner points to flip the shape diagonally as you draw.

- Drag across, up, or down to flip the shape horizontally or vertically as you draw.

For more information, see "Transforming objects" on page 168.

About adding images

You can place images in a title. This feature is particularly useful for adding a graphic to a title that serves as a template. You can either add the image as a graphic element or place it in a box to become part of the text. Adobe Premiere Elements accepts both bitmapped images and vector-based artwork (such as art created with Adobe Illustrator). However, Adobe Premiere Elements rasterizes vector-based art, converting it to a bitmapped version in the Monitor panel. By default, an inserted image appears at its original size. Once inserted into a title, you can modify the image's properties (such as scale) as you would other objects. Commands let you easily restore an image's original size and aspect ratio.

Note: Unlike text and graphic objects, images you add to titles aren't embedded as part of the title. Instead, the image references the source image file in the same way that items listed in the Media panel refer to source audio and video files.

To place an image into a title

1 Do one of the following:

- Click the Add Image button ![Add Image icon] at the bottom of the Properties panel.

- Right-click in the Monitor panel and choose Image > Add Image.

- Choose Title > Image > Add Image.

Adobe Premiere Elements imports the image at the size at which it was created.

2 Drag the image to the desired location in the Monitor panel. If necessary, you can adjust the size, opacity, rotation, and scale.

Note: Images acquired with a digital still camera tend to be much larger than a video project's screen size. To resize an image without distorting it, Shift-drag the image's corner handle or use the Title > Transform > Scale command.

For more information, see "About formatting text" on page 159.

To place an image in a text box

When you place an image in a text box, the image flows with the text as though it were a text character. It can have the same attributes as other characters, such as strokes.

1 Click and hold the Type Tool button **T**, and select either the Horizontal Type Tool or the Vertical Type Tool.

2 In the Monitor panel, click in a text box where you want to insert the image.

3 Do one of the following:

• Right-click the Monitor panel and choose Image > Insert Image Into Text.

• Choose Title > Image > Insert Image Into Text.

4 Select an image and click OK.

To restore an image to its original size or aspect ratio

❖ Select the image and do any of the following:

• Choose Title > Image > Restore Image Size.

• Choose Title > Image > Restore Image Aspect Ratio.

Note: If you want to use an image or moving video as a background only, superimpose the title on a clip of the image or video.

Arranging objects in titles

To change stacking order

When you create objects that overlap each other, you can control their stacking order by using the Arrange command.

1 Select the object you want to move.

2 Do one of the following:

• Right-click on the object and choose Arrange.

• Choose Title > Arrange.

3 Choose one of the following:

Bring To Front Brings the object to the top of the stacking order.

Bring Forward Switches the object with the object directly in front of it.

Send To Back Moves the object to the bottom of the stacking order.

Send Backward Switches the object with the object directly behind it.

Note: If your text or shape elements are densely stacked, it may be difficult to select an element within the stack. You can use the Title > Select or right-click > Select command to navigate easily through the stacked elements to reach the target element.

To center objects

❖ Select one or more objects and do any of the following:

- To center the object vertically, click the Vertical Center button ▮▮ .

- To center the object horizontally, click the Horizontal Center button ⬓ .

Aligning and distributing objects

Use the Align and Distribute commands to line up or evenly space selected objects within a title in the Monitor panel. You can align or distribute objects (text boxes, shapes, or both) along the vertical or horizontal axis. When you choose horizontal alignment, the selected objects align along the edge of the object's horizontal axis closest to the edge you choose. When you choose vertical alignment, the selected objects align along the edge of the object's vertical axis closest to the edge you choose. You can align or distribute objects by using a menu command or choosing Title > Align Objects and selecting the appropriate option.

When you align and distribute selected objects, keep the following in mind:

- An alignment option aligns selected objects to the object that most closely represents the new alignment. For example, for right-alignment, all selected objects align to the selected object that is farthest to the right.

- A distribution option evenly spaces selected objects between the two most extreme objects. For example, for a vertical distribution option, the selected objects are distributed between the highest and lowest selected objects.

- When you distribute objects of different sizes, the spaces between objects may not be uniform. For example, distributing objects by their centers creates equal space between the centers—but different-sized objects extend by different amounts into the space between objects. To create uniform spacing between selected objects, use the Horizontal Even Spacing or Vertical Even Spacing option.

To align objects

1 In the Monitor panel, Shift-click two or more objects or drag a marquee over them.

2 Do one of the following:

- Right-click any of the objects selected, and choose Align Objects.

- Choose Title > Align Objects.

3 Select the type of alignment you want.

To distribute objects

1 In the Monitor panel, Shift-click three or more objects or drag a marquee over them.

2 Do one of the following:

- Right-click any of the objects selected, and choose Distribute Objects.

- Choose Title > Distribute Objects.

3 Select the type of distribution you want.

Transforming objects

You have full flexibility in adjusting an object's position, rotation, scale, and opacity—attributes collectively referred to as *transform properties*. To transform an object, you can drag in the Monitor panel or choose a command from the Title menu.

To adjust an object's opacity

1 In the Monitor panel, Shift-click three or more objects or drag a marquee over them.

2 Do one of the following:

- Right-click any of the objects selected and choose Transform > Opacity.

- Choose Title > Transform > Opacity.

3 Type a new Opacity value, and click OK.

Note: The Opacity property setting adjusts the opacity of objects within a title. You can set the overall opacity of the entire title in the My Project panel as you would any video clip, using effects. (See "To create transparency" in Adobe Premiere Elements Help.)

To adjust the position of objects

1 In the Monitor panel, select one or more objects.

2 Do one of the following:

• Drag the selected object or objects to a new position.

• Choose Title > Transform > Position. Type new X and Y position values, and then click OK.

Note: X and Y position values correspond to a coordinate system in which the upper- left corner of the title is 0, 0. When you enter values for X and Y, Adobe Premiere Elements places the center of the selected object's bounding box at that point.

• Right-click the selected object or objects, and choose Transform > Position. Type new X and Y position values, and then click OK.

To scale objects

1 In the Monitor panel, select one or more objects.

2 Do one of the following:

• To scale the width, drag the object's left or right bounding box handles.

• To scale the height, drag the object's top or bottom bounding box handles.

• To constrain the object's proportions, press Shift as you drag the corner and bounding box handles.

• To scale and constrain the aspect ratio, press Shift as you drag the object's corner points.

• To scale from the center, Alt-drag the object's corner points.

• To set scale values in terms of percentages, choose Title > Transform > Scale, or right-click the object and choose Transform > Scale. Specify the values you want, and click OK.

Note: Dragging the bounding box handles of a text object created with the Type or Vertical Type tool changes its font size.

To change the rotation angle of objects

1 In the Monitor panel, select one or more objects.

2 Do one of the following:

• Place the cursor just outside the object's corner points. When the cursor becomes the Rotate icon ⤵, drag in the direction you want to adjust the angle. Shift-drag to constrain the rotation to 45˚ increments.

- Choose Title > Transform > Rotation, or right-click any of the selected objects and choose Transform > Rotation. Type a new rotation value, and then click OK.

Adding color and shadows

Color properties

You can specify the color properties of each object or group of objects you create in the Monitor panel. The Color Properties dialog box includes controls for setting the color and type of an object's stroke, fill, and shadow. You can save a combination of properties as a *style*. Styles appear as buttons in the Properties panel, allowing you to apply favorite property combinations to objects easily. Using styles helps you maintain consistency across multiple titles in a project.

For more information, see "To select and edit title text" on page 158 and "To create shapes" on page 164.

Setting an object's fill or stroke

You can use the Color Properties dialog box to set an object's fill and stroke. An object's *fill* property defines the area within the contours of the object: the space inside a graphic object or within the outline of each character of a text object. You can also edit the outline, or *stroke,* of an object to which you've applied a style containing a stroke. (See "About styles" on page 162.)

Note: The Fill and Stroke boxes in the Color Properties dialog box are enabled only if you've applied a preset style from Title Styles in the Properties panel to the object. These styles contain fills and strokes, which you can edit.

The Gradient menu includes options for how a fill or stroke color is applied. Color controls let you specify the color of a fill or stroke. Depending on the gradient type you select, additional color controls may appear.

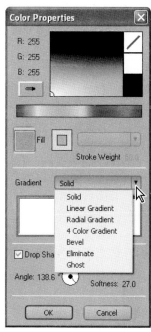

The Color Properties dialog box with Gradient pop-up menu open

To set the fill

1 Select an object, and in the Styles ![T] section of the Properties panel, select a style that includes a fill.

Note: *All preset styles in Title Styles contain a fill except the one in the upper-left corner of the panel.*

2 In the Monitor panel, click the Color Properties button ![icon].

3 In the Color Properties dialog box, select the Fill box ![icon].

4 From the Gradient menu, select the type of fill you want.

5 Use the Color Properties dialog box's color controls to select the color of the fill.

Note: *If you selected Linear Gradient, Radial Gradient, or 4-Color Gradient, color stop controls appear.*

To set the stroke

1 Select an object, and in the Styles 🔠 section of the Properties panel, select a style that includes one or more strokes.

Note: All preset styles in Styles contain a stroke except the one in the upper-left corner of the panel.

2 In the Monitor panel, click the Color Properties button ⬛ or right-click the object and choose Color Properties.

3 In the Color Properties dialog box, select the Stroke box ▣

4 From the Stroke menu, select the stroke you want to use.

5 For Stroke Weight, specify the stroke's thickness in pixels.

6 Use the color controls in the Color Properties dialog box to set the color of the stroke.

To set a fill or stroke color

1 In the Color Properties dialog box, select either of the following:

- To set the object's fill color, select the Fill box ⬛.
- To set the object's stroke color, select the Stroke box ▣.

Note: The Fill and Stroke boxes are available only if you've applied a preset style from the Title Styles in the Properties panel. All preset styles contain a fill and stroke except the one in the upper-left corner of the panel.

2 Choose an option in the Gradient menu.

3 If you choose a gradient or Bevel for Gradient, select the color stop you want to affect.

4 In the Color Properties dialog box, select either of the following:

- To make the selected fill or stroke transparent, click the No Color ◿ box.
- To set the color to pure white, click the white box.
- To set the color to pure black, click the black box.
- To set the hue, click the color you want in the rectangular spectrum.
- To set the saturation, click in the saturation box.
- To sample a color from the screen, select the Eyedropper tool ▰▰▰ and then click any point on the screen.

- To set the color numerically, set the R, G, and B values by dragging the value or clicking and entering a number.

5 If necessary, repeat steps 1-4, and then click OK.

Choosing a gradient type

Solid Creates a fill of uniform color.

Linear Gradient, Radial Gradient Linear Gradient creates a linear, two-color gradient fill. Radial Gradient creates a circular, two-color gradient fill.

The beginning and ending gradient colors are displayed, respectively, in the left and right boxes, or *color stops*. Select a color stop prior to choosing its color. Drag the color stops to adjust the transition smoothness between the colors.

The Angle option (available for Linear Gradient only) specifies the angle of the gradient. The Repeat option specifies the number of times to repeat the gradient pattern.

4-Color Gradient Creates a gradient fill composed of four colors, with a color emanating from each of the object's corners.

Four color stops specify the color that emanates from each corner of the object. Select a color stop prior to choosing its color.

Bevel Adds a beveled edge to the background. The object and bevel colors are displayed, respectively, in left and right color boxes. Select the box you want to adjust prior to setting its color. The Balance option specifies the percentage of the bevel that the shadow color occupies.

Eliminate Creates a transparent fill that casts no shadow. If the object has a stroke, the stroke may be visible.

Ghost Creates a transparent fill that casts a shadow. Specify shadow options in the Color Properties dialog box. (See "To create drop shadows" on page 174.)

 Eliminate and Ghost work best with objects that have shadows and strokes.

To create drop shadows

You can add a drop shadow to any object you create in the Monitor panel. A drop shadow can make an object appear three-dimensional and help make it stand out from the background image. For example, adding a drop shadow to text can make it more legible when superimposed on a complex background image.

1 Select an object and then click the Color Properties button .

2 In the Color Properties dialog box, select Drop Shadow.

3 Set any of the following:

Angle Specifies the angle of the shadow in relation to the object.

Distance Specifies the number of pixels that the shadow is offset from the object.

Softness Specifies how blurry or sharp the shadow appears.

Creating rolls and crawls

About rolling and crawling titles

Although static titles, graphics, and images may suffice for some projects, many others require titles that move across the screen. (Titles that move vertically are called *rolls*. Titles that move horizontally are called *crawls*.) Adobe Premiere Elements makes it easy to create smooth, expert rolls and crawls. It is also possible to make a title move along a custom path by keyframing locations for it at several points in time.

Note: The length of the title in the Timeline determines the speed of the roll or crawl. The more you increase the title clip length, the slower the movement.

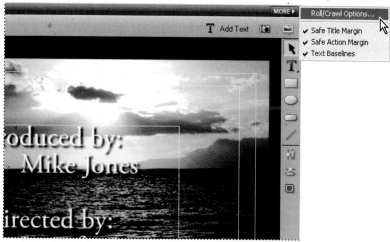

A title roll is commonly used for production credits.

To create a rolling or crawling title

1 Do one of the following:

• To create a rolling title, choose Title > New Title > Default Roll.

• To create a crawling title, choose Title > New Title > Default Crawl.

2 Create the text and graphic objects for the title. Use the Monitor panel's scroll bar to view offscreen areas of the title. When the title is added to the My Project panel, the hidden offscreen areas roll or crawl into view.

3 In the Monitor panel, click the More button and choose Roll/Crawl Options.

4 Specify the appropriate Direction and Timing options, and then click OK.

Note: You can specify a direction for crawling titles only. Rolling titles always move from the bottom to the top of the screen.

To convert a title from one type to another

1 Select the title you want to convert in the Monitor panel.

2 Click the Roll/Crawl Options button ≣↑ at the bottom of the Properties panel.

3 For Title Type, specify the kind of title you want and, if desired, specify Direction and Timing options. Click OK. (See "Roll/Crawl options" on page 176.)

4 Click in the Monitor panel outside of the box to save the converted title.

Note: Boxes created for rolling or crawling extend into offscreen areas when you convert a rolling or crawling title into a static title.

For more information, see "To create a new still title" on page 152.

Roll/Crawl options

Start Offscreen Specifies that the roll or crawl begins out of view and moves into view.

End Offscreen Specifies that the roll or crawl continues until the objects are out of view.

Preroll Specifies the number of frames that play before the roll or crawl begins.

Ease-In Specifies the number of frames that the title rolls or crawls at a slowly increasing speed until the title reaches the playback speed.

Ease-Out Specifies the number of frames that the title rolls or crawls at a slowly decreasing speed until the roll or crawl completes.

Postroll Specifies the number of frames that play after the roll or crawl completes.

Crawl Left and Crawl Right Specifies the direction in which a crawl moves.

For more information, see "To create a new still title" on page 152.

Exporting and importing titles

To export a title file

You can export a title from Adobe Premiere Elements to a file for use in another Adobe Premiere Elements project.

1 In the Media panel, click the Available Media button 🎞 .

2 In the Media panel, select the title you want to export as a separate file.

3 Choose File > Export > Title.

4 Specify the name and location for the saved title file and click Save.

To import a title file

You can import a title into a project that was exported from another Adobe Premiere Elements project.

1 In the task bar, click the Get Media From button and choose Files and Folders.

2 Select a title and click Open.

Note: To display only title files in the Add Media dialog box, choose Adobe Title Designer (.prtl) from the Files of Type menu.

For more information, see "File types you can import" on page 66 and "File types available for export" on page 215.

Chapter 11: Adding and mixing audio

Audio basics

Enhancing movies with audio

At least half of your movie's impact comes from its use of sound, and Adobe Premiere Elements provides the tools you need to deliver a high-quality sound mix. You can narrate clips while previewing them in real time. You can add a soundtrack to your movie, and trim it to the proper length. You can set the overall volume levels of clips and the relative volume levels within and among them. Finally, you can remove unwanted noises and add various effects to the sounds in your movie.

For more information, see "To apply an audio effect" on page 135 and "To preview an audio effect" on page 136.

Adding narrations and soundtracks

To set up for narration

For best results, confirm that your microphone is working correctly with your computer and Adobe Premiere Elements before narrating a clip.

1 Plug a computer microphone into your computer's microphone jack.

2 Test the microphone through the Windows Sound Hardware Test Wizard. Check the Windows documentation for instructions.

3 In Adobe Premiere Elements, choose Edit > Preferences > Audio Hardware.

4 From the Default Device menu, select your computer's sound device. Click OK.

To narrate a clip

Using your computer's microphone, you can narrate clips while previewing them in the Monitor panel. Adobe Premiere Elements will add your narrations to the Narration sound track visible in either view of the My Project panel.

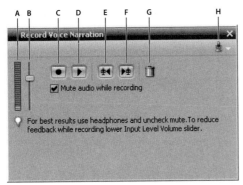

Record voice narration
A. Volume indicator **B.** Input Volume Level slider **C.** Record **D.** Play **E.** Go To Previous Narration Clip **F.** Go To Next Narration Clip **G.** Delete Present Narration **H.** Microphone source

1 In the task bar, click the Edit Movie button 🎬 .

2 Do one of the following:

• In the Sceneline, select the clip you want to narrate. Then, in the Monitor panel, drag the current-time indicator ⊤ to the point at which you want the narration to begin.

• In the Timeline, drag the current-time indicator ⍦ in the Timeline to the point at which you want the narration to begin.

3 In the My Project panel, click the Add Narration button 🎤 .

The Record Voice Narration window appears.

4 In the Record Voice Narration window, click the Mic Source button 🎤 and select your sound device from the popup menu.

5 For best results, turn off your computer speakers to prevent feedback. To monitor sound while you narrate, plug headphones into your computer and deselect Mute Audio While Recording.

Note: If your speakers are turned on, get as close to the microphone as possible, and keep the microphone as far away from the speakers as possible to prevent feedback.

6 Speak into the microphone at a conversational volume, and raise or lower the Input Volume Level slider until your loudest words light up the orange part of the meters.

7 Click the Record button 💿 .

8 Near the top of the Record Voice Narration window, a timer appears next to Start Recording In. Wait while it counts down. When Start Recording In changes to Recording, speak your narration as the selected clip plays.

9 When you finish narrating, click the Stop button ⏹ .

Adobe Premiere Elements adds an audio clip containing your narration to the Media panel and to the Narration track in the My Project panel (below the selected clip).

Note: *If you do not click the Stop button, Adobe Premiere Elements automatically stops recording at the start of the next file in the Narration track. If there is none, it stops 30 seconds past the end of the last clip in the My Project panel.*

10 To preview your recording, click the Go To Previous Narration button 🔙 . Then click the Play Present Narration button ▶ .

11 To continue recording from the point at which you stopped, click the Record button 💿 again.

This will overwrite any narrations already in the Narration track at that point.

12 Click the Pause button ⏸ at any time to stop the preview.

💡 *In the Sceneline, a microphone icon 🎙 appears beneath any clip you've narrated.*

For more information, see "To set up for narration" on page 179 and "Using the Sceneline view of the My Project panel" on page 81.

To replace or discard a narration

1 Do one of the following:

- If using the Sceneline, select the clip containing the narration you want to change. Then, in the Monitor panel, drag the current-time indicator 🔻 to the location where the old narration begins.

- If using the Timeline, drag the current-time indicator 🔻 in the Timeline to the location where the old narration begins.

2 Then click the Add Narration button .

3 In the Record Voice Narration window, do either of the following:

- To replace the narration, click the Record button ⬤ . This overwrites the existing recording with the new one.

- To discard a narration, click the Delete Present Narration button 🗑 .

The old narration clip is removed from the My Project panel, but remains in the Media panel.

To add audio to the Soundtrack

To complement the sounds embedded in your video clips and any narration you record, you can add audio clips to the Soundtrack track, visible in either view of the My Project panel. These clips typically contain background music or recordings of environmental sound.

To prepare, copy the desired audio files from devices, websites, or disks and add them to your project.

Important: Use only files for which you hold the copyright or which you have permission to use from the copyright holder.

1 In the Media panel, click the Available Media button 🎞 .

2 Drag an audio clip from the Media panel and drop it into the Soundtrack track of the My Project panel where you want to the audio clip to begin.

For more information, see "Adding audio files" on page 68.

To preview a Soundtrack clip

1 In the My Project panel, select an audio clip in the Soundtrack track.

2 Do one of the following:

- Click the Play button ▶ in the Monitor panel.

- Press the spacebar.

Adobe Premiere Elements will preview the Soundtrack audio clip along with any audio and video clips above it in the My Project panel.

3 To stop the preview do one of the following:

- Click the Pause button ⏸ in the Monitor.

- Press the spacebar.

Mixing audio

About audio mixing

Fundamentally, mixing audio involves adjusting volume levels so that they maintain a good range within each clip, and then adjusting them in proportion to other clips used in the movie. For example, you might first adjust the volume of a narration clip so that there is little variance between its softest and loudest sections; then raise the narration's overall volume so that it is clearly audible over background sounds or music included in other clips. Additionally, mixing can involve making changes to your movie's audio by applying effects to it.

Mixing audio in Adobe Premiere Elements can include any combination of the following tasks:

- Setting Audio Gain for a clip as a whole.

- Boosting soft sections of a clip to make sure they are heard, and lowering loud sections so they don't become distorted.

- Adjusting a clip's volume in relation to sounds on other sound tracks.

- Fading (increasing or decreasing) the volume levels of clips over time.

- Combining up to 99 audio tracks into a rich array of music, dialog, and sound effects.

- Using audio effects to remove noise, enhance frequency response and dynamic range, sweeten the sound, or create interesting audio distortions, such as reverb.

For more information, see "To apply an audio effect" on page 135 and "To preview an audio effect" on page 136.

Adjusting volume levels

In Adobe Premiere Elements, volume changes are measured in decibels. A level of 0.0 dB is the original volume (not silence). Changing the level to a negative number reduces the volume, and changing the level to a positive number increases the volume.

You use the Volume graph—the yellow line running horizontally across the audio track of each clip—to control the clip's volume. By dragging the Volume graph up or down, you can, for example, make the volume of a clip match that of its neighbors, or mute it entirely.

Consider the following guidelines when adjusting volume levels:

- If you combine particularly loud audio clips on multiple tracks, *clipping* (a staccato distortion) may occur. To avoid clipping, reduce volume levels.

- If you need to adjust the volume separately in different parts of a clip (for example, one person's voice is faint, while later another's is too loud) you can use keyframes to vary the volume throughout the clip. (See "To display keyframes in the Properties panel" in Adobe Premiere Elements Help.)

- If the original level of a clip is much too high or low, you can change the input level. (See "To adjust the input level of a clip" on page 185.) However, adjusting the input level will not remove any distortion that may have resulted from recording the clip too high. In those cases, it is best to re-record the clip.

Audio Meters panel

The Audio Meters panel displays the overall volume level of the clips as you play them from the My Project panel. If the meter's red clipping indicators turn on, lower the volume of one or more clips. The peak indicators show the peak volume reached while playing the movie. Generally, you want the peak to be between 0 and -6 dB.

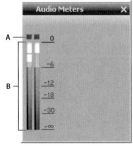

Audio Meters panel
A. Clipping indicators B. Peak volume indicators

To view the Audio Meters panel

❖ Select Window > Audio Meters.

To adjust volume

You can adjust clip volume directly on an audio track in the Timeline view of the My Project panel.

Note: You can also raise and lower volume with keyframes. (See "To add keyframes in the Properties panel" in Adobe Premiere Elements Help.)

1 Click the Timeline button ![icon] in the My Project panel.

2 To resize an audio track for better visibility, position the pointer between two tracks in the track header area so that the Height Adjustment icon ![icon] appears, and then drag up or down.

3 In the Timeline, select Volume in the upper left corner of the clip. Then, select Volume > Clip Volume.

Volume menu

4 Position the pointer over the Volume graph: the yellow line running horizontally across the audio track of the clip. The pointer changes to the white double-arrow icon ![icon].

5 Drag up or down to adjust the level uniformly. Click and drag any existing keyframes to move them.

As you drag, the decibel level is displayed. A positive number indicates an increase in volume; a negative number indicates a decrease.

Dragging the Volume graph changes the clip's volume.

To adjust the input level of a clip

If the original volume of the clip is much too high or low, you must change the input level, or *gain*, before making adjustments to the output levels. However, if the level of source audio was set too low when it was recorded, increasing the gain might simply amplify noise.

For best results, record audio at a high volume level that is not so high as to cause distortion. Without adjustment, well-recorded audio peaks between 0 and -6dB in the Audio Meters panel. Recording audio above 0 dB may result in clipping.

1 Click the Timeline button ▣ in the My Project panel.

2 In the Timeline, select the clip.

3 Choose Clip > Audio Options > Audio Gain.

4 Do one of the following, and then click OK:

- Type a gain value (0 dB equals the clip's original gain).

- Click Normalize to automatically boost gain where it's too quiet or reduce gain where it's too loud. Adobe Premiere Elements displays the amount required to reach maximum gain without clipping.

To mute a clip

1 Click the Timeline button in the My Project panel.

2 Do one of the following:

- If the clip is linked to video, Alt-click the audio track of the clip in the Timeline to select just the audio portion.

- If the clip is not linked to video, click the clip to select it.

3 Choose Clip > Enable. (When you disable a clip, the check mark disappears next to the option in the clip menu, and the clip name dims in the track.)

To fade volume in or out

1 Select an audio clip in the My Project panel.

2 In the Properties panel, click either the Fade In button ◢ or Fade Out button ◣ .

Fade In adds a keyframe at the very beginning of the clip where it sets the volume to -∞ dB (silence) and another after it where it retains the volume already set for the clip at that point. Fade Out adds a keyframe at the end of the clip where it sets the volume to -∞ dB and another before it where it retains the volume already set for the clip at that point.

> *If the audio clip is linked to video, you can right-click either portion of the clip and choose Fade > Fade In Audio And Video or Fade Out Audio And Video. You can also fade the volume of one clip out while fading the volume of another clip in by dragging either of the Crossfade audio transitions to the cut line between the clips.*

Chapter 12: Creating DVDs

DVD basics

Types of DVDs

DVDs are a great way to share your video with family and friends. The small, lightweight DVD discs are easy to pack and mail, making them an ideal medium for delivering your movies.

By using the Adobe Premiere Elements menu templates and their automated features, you can create professional-looking DVDs quickly and easily.

The first step in creating a DVD is deciding on the type of DVD you want to create.

Auto-play DVD These DVDs work best for presenting single movies that you will generally want to view from start to finish. Auto-play DVDs begin playing when inserted into a DVD player. These DVDs contain no menus and are the easiest to create—you simply export the movie to a DVD. There is no navigation, although you can skip from scene to scene using a remote control. To skip scenes, however, you must add DVD markers. Markers let you skip forward or back through the movie by using the Next and Previous buttons on a DVD player's remote control.

Menu-based DVD with scenes menu These DVDs are best for presenting single long movies that play well from start to finish, but that also contain scenes that you might want to access from a submenu. From the main menu, you can choose to play the whole movie or go instead to a scenes menu. The scenes menu lets you navigate to scenes within the movie. You generally set up the project so that each scene represents an interesting point in the movie; however, it is also possible to start a scene whenever a certain amount of play time has elapsed, or anywhere else you'd like.

Menu-based DVD with several movie selections These DVDs are best for presenting a set of individual movies that you don't want to combine into a single movie. For example, in a wedding DVD, you might want to present the preparations, the ceremony, and the reception as separate movies. Each will have its own button on the main menu.

Note: The available menus are set to the project's aspect ratio. For example, if the project's aspect ratio is set for widescreen playback, the menus also play back in widescreen. (See "About project settings and presets" on page 41.)

For more information, see "About Video CD formats" on page 228.

Understanding the DVD creation process

To create a DVD, either with or without menus, click the Create DVD button ⊙. This opens the DVD workspace.

You create a DVD with menus by using the Adobe Premiere Elements menu templates. The templates are predesigned menus that come in a variety of themes and styles. The buttons on the templates automatically link to DVD markers placed in the movie. Adobe Premiere Elements creates the menus dynamically based on the markers you've placed, adding additional menus if needed. You normally add DVD markers in the My Project panel before you select a DVD template, but you can add, move, or delete DVD markers after choosing a template as well. Adobe Premiere Elements automatically adjusts the DVD menus to match the markers.

Working with DVD markers

Understanding DVD markers

You can add DVD markers to mark additional movies, chapters, scenes, and stop points in the DVD after you have completely finished editing your movie. Adobe Premiere Elements creates a DVD menu based on the DVD markers. If you later rearrange clips in the My Project panel, the DVD markers remain in their original locations, so you might have to update their locations and edit their names to keep them relevant to the movie.

Note: Do not confuse DVD markers with clip markers and timeline markers. Although they all mark locations within the clip or movie, Adobe Premiere Elements uses DVD markers to link the video frame in the My Project panel to buttons on DVD menus. Clip markers and timeline markers help you position and trim clips.

The type of DVD markers you add to the My Project panel depends on how you want your viewers to access the video. In general, use these guidelines:

• Use Main Menu Markers (and Stop Markers) to divide the video into separate movies. Buttons on the main menu link to Main Menu Markers.

- Use Scene Markers (without Stop Markers) when you want the movie to play from start to finish, and also want your viewer to be able to jump ahead to specific scenes. Scene buttons link to Scene Markers and appear on scene menus one after another (not grouped by movie).

- Use Stop Markers to designate the end of a movie. When the DVD player reaches a Stop Marker, it returns to the Main Menu. If you add a Stop Marker to the My Project panel, a DVD player doesn't play the movie from start to finish. Therefore, you generally add Stop Markers only if you've divided your video into separate movies, and don't need to play the clips in the My Project panel from beginning to end.

Note: You can use both Main Menu Markers and Scene Markers in a movie. However, you must remember that once the DVD player encounters a Stop Marker, it returns to the Main Menu, not the menu from which it was called.

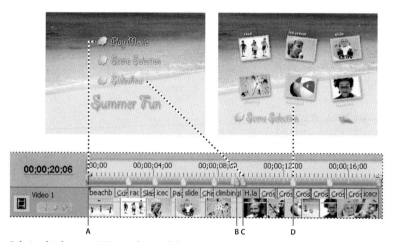

Relationship between DVD markers and the menu templates
A. Media Start B. Stop Marker C. Main Menu Marker D. Scene Marker

Main Menu Markers

You manually place DVD Main Menu Markers to indicate the beginning of each movie that you want listed on the main menu of your DVD. If the Main Menu template you select contains extra buttons (buttons other than the Play Movie or Scenes buttons), those buttons link to the Main Menu Markers and play from each marker until reaching a Stop Marker or the end of the media in the My Project panel. If the main menu does not contain enough

Main Menu Marker buttons, Adobe Premiere Elements duplicates the main menu and adds a Next button on the primary main menu. If you have no Main Menu Markers in your movie, Adobe Premiere Elements omits the extra buttons from the main menu.

If you use Main Menu Markers, choose a template with at least three Main Menu Marker buttons. (The first button, Play Movie, plays the movie from beginning to end. The second, Scenes, links to Scenes Menu 1.) Button information is displayed in the Template Details section of the DVD Templates dialog box.

Important: The Play button on the main menu automatically links to the starting point of the time ruler, so you don't need to place a Main Menu Marker there.

Duplicate menus created when movie contains more Main Menu Markers than buttons on template
A. Next button leads to duplicate menu B. Previous button returns user to main menu

For more information, see "To add a Main Menu Marker or Scene Marker" on page 193 and "To choose a DVD menu template" on page 199.

Scene Markers

You can add DVD Scene Markers automatically or manually where desired. Adobe Premiere Elements uses Scene Markers to create a scene menu, which is accessible from the Scenes button on the DVD main menu. If you have no Scene Markers in the My Project panel, Adobe Premiere Elements omits the Scenes button and the scenes menu.

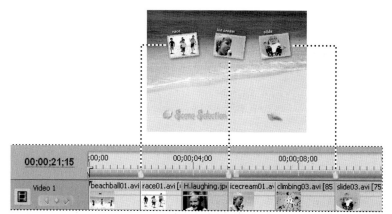

Scene Markers map directly to buttons on scenes menu.

Adding Scene Markers automatically

The Auto-Generate DVD Markers command places DVD Scene Markers for you. It gives you three placement options: at each scene, at a specified interval, or at an interval determined by the number of markers you specify. When placing at each scene, the command sets a Scene Marker at the boundaries between clips, not at the ends of transitions, on the Video 1 track. You get the best results when each scene in your movie is a separate clip, and all the clips you want marked are on the Video 1 track. If your movie consists of multiple clips that overlay each other, you might prefer to place Scene Markers manually or place them at set intervals. Sometimes you can save time if you let Adobe Premiere Elements initially place Scene Markers, which you can clean up later as necessary.

Note: Adobe Premiere Elements places only one scene marker at the beginning of any series of still images in the My Project panel.

If you don't like the placement of a DVD marker, you can simply drag it in the time ruler to a different location. DVD markers are not tied to the video. If you later edit the video, you may need to move the markers or regenerate them so that they match the new edit points.

Sample movie with automatically placed Scene Marker

Automatically placed Scene Markers do not have names, so the buttons on the Scene menu remain as named in the template. To customize the buttons, you can either name the markers after they are placed or rename the buttons after you select the template.

For more information, see "To edit a DVD marker" on page 196 and "To edit menu text and buttons" on page 202.

To add Scene Markers automatically

1 In the My Project panel, click the Timeline button ⬛ .

2 Choose DVD > Auto-Generate DVD Markers.

3 In the Automatically Set DVD Scene Markers dialog box, select how you want the markers placed, entering a value if required:

- At Each Scene places a Scene Marker at each edit point (cut) between clips on the Video 1 track.

- Every _ Minutes places Scene Markers at the interval you specify. (This option is only available when the movie contains several minutes of footage.)

- Total Markers spaces the number of markers you specify evenly across the entire range of clips in the Timeline.

4 If the Timeline contains existing DVD markers that you no longer want, select Clear Existing DVD Markers. (When you clear the markers, you clear the marker names and thumbnail offsets associated with each one.)

5 Click OK.

Adobe Premiere Elements adds Scene Markers to the Timeline view of the My Project panel, underneath the time ruler.

Adding DVD markers manually

When you manually add markers, you can name them as you place them. The name you choose appears as the label for a button in the main menu or scenes menu.

On some templates, the menu buttons include thumbnail images of the video to which they are linked. By default, the thumbnail displays the frame visible at the position of the marker. However, the default frame does not necessarily represent the best frame for a button. In the DVD Marker dialog box, you can change the frame a thumbnail displays. For example, for the button representing a scene of a day at the beach, you might want to change the button image to a close-up of the kids splashing in the water rather than the frame marked by the DVD marker. Choosing a thumbnail for a button does not change the start point of the video to which the button is linked. Because you may not know now what type of menu you'll choose and whether it will contain thumbnail images, you can always change the thumbnail after you choose the menu.

For information on changing the thumbnail after selecting a template, see "To edit a DVD marker" on page 196. For more information about the type of marker to use, see "To customize menu backgrounds" on page 203

To add a Main Menu Marker or Scene Marker

1 In the Timeline view of the My Project panel, move the current-time indicator ♆ to the location where you want to set the marker.

Note: The Play button on each main menu template automatically links to the start point of the time ruler. You don't have to place a marker there unless you want it listed in the scenes menu.

2 Click the Add DVD Scene button 🎬 just above the time ruler.

💡 *To quickly place a marker, you can also drag a marker from the DVD Marker button to the desired location in the time ruler.*

3 In the DVD Marker dialog box, type a name for the marker in the text box. Text in this box doesn't wrap, so to place text on multiple lines, press Ctrl+Enter for each new line. Keep the name of the marker short so that it fits in the menu and doesn't overlap another button. (You can adjust the name later, after you select a template.)

4 In the Marker Type menu, select the type of marker you want to set.

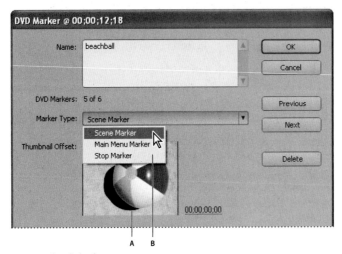

DVD Marker dialog box
A. *Thumbnail of frame at the marker* **B.** *Marker type*

5 Do one of the following to set the appearance of the button thumbnail:

• To select a still image for the button thumbnail in the menu, drag the Thumbnail Offset timecode to the frame with the image you want. Do not select the Motion Menu Button option. When you create the DVD, the image appears in the menu. (This thumbnail is for the menu display only. When you click the button on the DVD, the video starts playing at the marker location.)

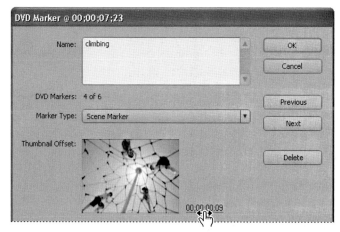

Dragging the Thumbnail Offset timecode

- To play video in the DVD's menu button, select Motion Menu Button. When you select this option for a Main Menu Marker or Scene Marker, the corresponding button in the menu becomes animated.

6 Click OK.

The marker is added to the Timeline view of the My Project panel, below the time ruler. A Main Menu Marker is blue; a Scene Marker is green.

To add a Stop Marker

1 In the Timeline view of the My Project panel, move the current-time indicator 🚩 to the end of the video or scene.

2 Click the Add DVD Scene button 🔘 just above the time ruler.

3 In the DVD Marker dialog box, select Stop Marker from the Marker Type menu.

4 Click OK.

The marker is added to the Timeline below the time ruler.

To move a DVD marker

Whether you placed a marker automatically or manually, you can move DVD markers simply by dragging.

1 If the Timeline is not visible, click the Edit Movie button ![icon] in the task bar.

2 In the My Project panel, click the Timeline button ![icon].

3 In the Timeline, drag the DVD marker you want to move to the desired scene or movie.

To find a DVD marker

1 In the My Project panel, click the Timeline button ![icon].

2 Do one of the following:

- To find the first DVD marker to the right or left of the current-time indicator, choose DVD > Go To DVD Marker > Next or Previous.

- To find any DVD marker in the Timeline, click the Add DVD Scene button ![icon] to the left of the time ruler. In the DVD Marker dialog box, click Previous or Next until you find the marker you want.

- To find a DVD marker linked to a specific button, click the thumbnail of the menu at the bottom of the DVD Layout panel, right click the button, and choose Reveal Marker In Timeline.

Note: When you have found a DVD marker in the DVD Marker dialog box, you may edit the details of the marker, or delete it by clicking the Delete button.

For more information, see "To edit a DVD marker" on page 196 and "To delete a DVD marker" on page 197.

To edit a DVD marker

After you place a DVD marker, you can change its name, type (Scene, Main Menu, or Stop), and the thumbnail image displayed in a thumbnail button on a menu. The marker names become the button names in the main menu or scenes menu.

1 In the Timeline view of the My Project panel, double-click the DVD marker you want to edit, or locate the marker using the Previous and Next buttons. (See "To find a DVD marker" on page 196.)

2 In the DVD Marker dialog box, do any of the following, and then click OK:

• Type a name for the marker in the text box. Text in this box doesn't wrap, so to place the name on multiple lines, press Ctrl+Enter for each new line. Keep the name short so that it fits in the menu and doesn't overlap another button. (You can adjust the name later, after you select a template.)

• Select the type of marker you want to set in the Marker Type menu.

• Drag the Thumbnail Offset timecode to select the image you want displayed in the button thumbnail in the menu. If you choose a menu with thumbnail images, the image you select displays in the menu when you create the DVD. (This thumbnail is for the menu display only; the video linked to the button starts at the marker location.)

To delete a DVD marker

You can delete individual DVD markers or clear all markers from the My Project panel at once. If you have edited your movie since you first selected DVD menu templates, you may find it is easier to delete all the markers rather than drag them to new positions.

Note: If you have already selected a DVD template, deleting a DVD marker also deletes the button associated with the marker from the main menu or scenes menu.

❖ Do one of the following:

• In the My Project panel, click the Timeline button 🗔 . Position the current-time indicator 🚩 over the DVD marker that you want to delete. (You may need to zoom into the time ruler to find the marker.) Choose DVD > Clear DVD Marker > DVD Marker At Current Time Indicator.

• To find and delete a marker, double-click any marker. In the DVD marker dialog box, click the Previous and Next buttons to find the marker, and then click the Delete button.

• To delete all DVD markers at once, choose DVD > Clear DVD Marker > All DVD Markers.

If you change your mind or make a mistake, you can undo recent deletions. Choose Edit > Undo. The DVD marker reappears in the My Project panel.

Creating DVDs without menus

About auto-play DVDs

An auto-play DVD contains no menus. Instead, it plays automatically when you insert the DVD into a DVD player. However, you can set DVD markers so that the Next and Previous buttons on the DVD remote control jump to specific points in the movie. Because an auto-play DVD does not distinguish between Main Menu Markers and Scene Markers, you can add either type of marker for chapter points.

Note: *Auto-play DVDs ignore Stop Markers.*

For more information, see "To add Scene Markers automatically" on page 192 and "To add a Main Menu Marker or Scene Marker" on page 193.

To create an auto-play DVD

1 In the task bar, click Create DVD ⬛ , and do not drag a DVD Template onto the DVD Layout panel.

2 To preview the DVD and test your markers, click Preview DVD and use the Previous Scene button ⬛ , the Next Scene button ⬛ , and the Play button ⬛ .

3 Close the Preview DVD dialog box and click Burn DVD.

4 In the Burn DVD dialog box, select the desired options. Then, click Burn.

For more information, see "About burning DVDs" on page 208.

Creating DVDs with menus

About DVD menu templates

You create a menu-based DVD by using the predesigned menu templates included in Adobe Premiere Elements. Each template includes Main Menu 1 and Scenes Menu 1 templates. Some templates also include background audio and video. The templates automatically link menu buttons with DVD markers in the My Project panel.

In the templates, the main menus contain a minimum of two buttons: one to play the movie, the other to display a scenes menu. The main menus in some templates also contain additional buttons designed to jump to other movies marked in the My Project panel. The scenes menus generally contain buttons with both an identifying label and a thumbnail image from the scene. (The thumbnail on the menu displays a still image from the video, not the video itself.)

Some templates include audio, video, or both in the background and are identified by a letter before their name: (A) indicates audio background, (V) indicates video background, and (AV) indicates both audio and video.

You're not limited to the prebuilt appearance of a menu template. You can personalize it for your project by changing fonts, colors, backgrounds, and layout, but these template changes apply only to the current project; you cannot save template changes in Adobe Premiere Elements. However, you can create a custom template in Photoshop Elements, and then add it to the Adobe Premiere Elements template choices.

You can make changes to both the menu appearance and buttons using a combination of the Properties panel, the DVD Layout panel, and the DVD Marker dialog box. The Properties panel provides more advanced ways to personalize your menu.

For more information, see "To switch to a different DVD menu template" "To specify text settings," and "To change from a menu-based DVD to an auto-play DVD" in Adobe Premiere Elements Help.

For more information, see "Creating Photoshop files in Adobe Premiere Elements" on page 243.

To choose a DVD menu template

When you choose a DVD menu template, don't be concerned if it doesn't have enough menu buttons to match each DVD marker in the movie. Adobe Premiere Elements creates additional menus and buttons as needed.

When you select a template, the button text on the menus changes to the names you've given the DVD markers. If you added the markers automatically or haven't named the markers, you can name them after you select the template, as well as change the title of the menu. If you don't provide marker names, the buttons remain as named in the template.

You usually add DVD markers before you select a DVD template, but it isn't required. You can add, move, or delete DVD markers after choosing a template. Adobe Premiere Elements dynamically adjusts the DVD menus to match the markers, adding or deleting buttons as necessary.

1 Click the Create DVD button .

This will open the DVD Layout panel and the DVD Templates view of the Media panel.

2 In DVD Templates, select a template with a theme matching that of your project. If you have used Main Menu Markers, choose a template with at least three buttons on the main menu. (The first button is labelled Play Movie and the second, Scenes. Additional buttons link to DVD markers in the My Project panel.)

3 Click OK.

Adobe Premiere Elements links the buttons to the DVD markers in the My Project panel and inserts the DVD marker names for the button text.

4 You may be asked whether you want to add DVD Scene Markers automatically. If you click Yes, select one of the following options, and then click OK:

At Each Scene Places a Scene Marker at each edit point (cut) between clips on the Video 1 track.

Every _ Minutes Places Scene Markers at the interval you specify. (This option is available only when the movie contains several minutes of footage.)

Total Markers Spaces your markers evenly across the entire range of clips in the My Project panel.

Note: If you choose not to add markers automatically at this time, you can add them later. Adobe Premiere Elements updates DVD menus dynamically, adding Main Marker buttons or scenes menus and buttons if you add DVD markers.

5 Click the thumbnail of the menu on the bottom of the DVD Layout panel to view a menu. If necessary, use the scroll bar to scroll to the thumbnail you want to view, or resize the panel so that the thumbnails are displayed side by side.

6 (Optional) After you choose a template in the DVD Layout panel, you can customize the menu, preview the DVD, or burn the DVD.

For more information, see "Preview DVD panel" on page 207 and "To add a Main Menu Marker or Scene Marker" on page 193.

To change the placement and size of menu items

1 At the bottom of the DVD Layout panel, click the thumbnail of the menu you want to change.

2 Do any of the following:

- To resize a menu item, select it in the DVD Layout panel. A rectangle (called a *bounding box*) with eight selection points appears around the item. Drag any selection point to resize the item. Alternatively, you can use the – (minus) or = (equal) keys on your keyboard to resize the item proportionately in all directions. The equal key enlarges the item.

Drag a selection point on the bounding box to resize a menu item.

- To move a menu item, select the item and drag it. Alternatively, you can use the arrow keys on your keyboard to move the item in any direction.

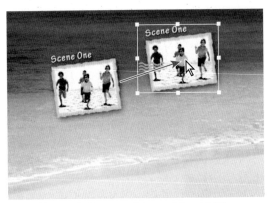

Original location (left) compared to moved item (right)

To edit menu text and buttons

After you select the DVD template, you can change menu text or the appearance of any of the main menu or scene buttons. You can also delete any button. Because the buttons are linked to the DVD markers, deleting a button deletes the marker that generated it.

1 At the bottom of the DVD Layout panel, click the thumbnail of the menu you want to change.

2 To edit text or buttons not connected to markers, double-click the menu title or button and edit the text in the Change Text dialog box. To use multiple lines, press Ctrl+Enter for each new line. Click OK.

3 To edit buttons connected to DVD markers, double-click the text or button, do any of the following in the DVD Marker dialog box, and then click OK:

- To rename the marker (and the button in the menu), type a new name and click OK. To use multiple lines, press Ctrl+Enter for each new line. Keep the name short so that it fits in the menu and doesn't overlap another button.

- To select the image you want displayed in the button thumbnail in the menu, drag the Thumbnail Offset timecode, and click OK. (This thumbnail is for the menu display only. If you select the Motion Menu Button option, the video linked to the button starts at the marker location.)

- To delete a button, click Delete. Adobe Premiere Elements deletes the marker from the My Project panel and the button from the DVD menu. Alternatively, you can select the button's marker in the Timeline, and press the Delete key.

For more information, see "To add a Main Menu Marker or Scene Marker" on page 193 and "To animate buttons" on page 205.

About motion menus

A menu can include sound and motion. You can replace the entire background of a menu with a video file, or use a still background and add background audio. A video can serve as a moving backdrop to a menu or provide all the visual elements of the menu, except for the button highlighting. The video can include, for example, a moving background, scrolling credits, and even the button images.

How long the video background or audio play depends on the duration of the menu. The duration of a single loop of background audio and video must be 30 seconds or less.

To customize menu backgrounds

You can personalize your menu background with either a video clip, a video clip with audio, an audio clip, a still image, or a still image with audio.

1 At the bottom of the DVD Layout panel, click the thumbnail of the menu you want to change.

2 Select a clip or still image in the Media panel and do either of the following:

- Drag the clip or still image to the background of the menu in the DVD Layout panel.

- Drag the clip or still image to the drop zone in the Properties panel. Alternatively, you can click Browse to locate a clip on your hard drive, or select a clip in the My Project panel. If the clip contains both video and audio, you can drag it to either drop zone.

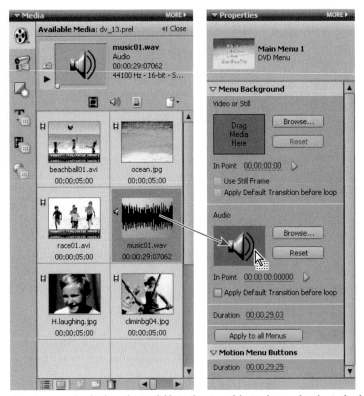

*Dragging an audio clip from the Available Media view of the Media panel to the Audio drop zone in the
Properties panel for a menu. Note Video Or Still drop zone above the Audio drop zone.*

Note: *When both video and audio are set and you replace one of the clips, the other clip
remains set, unless you select background video that also contains audio. In that case, the
background audio overrides the existing audio.*

3 Specify settings in the Properties panel:

Reset Sets the background to the original template background.

In Point Sets the In Point of the video or audio clip. Drag the timecode to the desired frame.

Play Plays media in the thumbnail. The icon changes from the Play button ▷ to the Pause
button ▏▏. Click the Pause button to stop the playback and set the In Point of the
background.

Use Still Frame Sets the current frame in the video clip as a still background image. Drag the timecode to set the frame.

Apply Default Transition Before Loop Adds the transition you've set as the default each time the video starts from the beginning. (See "To specify a default transition" on page 127.)

Duration Sets the duration of background video or audio from the In points.

Apply To All Menus Applies the background to all DVD menus.

To animate buttons

You can add video to main menu and scene menu buttons if the template contains buttons that display a thumbnail.

1 At the bottom of the DVD Layout panel, click the thumbnail of the menu you want to change.

2 Select a button in the DVD Layout panel.

3 In the Properties panel, select Motion Menu Button.

Scenes menu with button selected (left) and Motion Menu Button selected in Properties panel (right)

4 Set the In point where you want the clip to start playing when the menu is displayed. You can either use the Play/Stop button to view the clip in the thumbnail, or edit the In Point timecode field.

5 To set the duration for the clip to play, click the background of the menu, and then in the Properties panel under Motion Menu Button, edit the Duration timecode field.

Note: *The duration you set for a motion menu button applies to all motion menu buttons on the DVD.*

Previewing DVDs

Preview DVD panel

It's always a good idea to preview a DVD before you burn it. The Preview DVD panel contains controls that mimic those on a DVD remote control. By using these controls, you can test each button on the menus and view the video to which they link. You can preview a DVD in a window or full-screen.

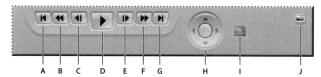

Preview DVD navigation controls
A. Previous Scene B. Rewind C. Frame Backward D. Play E. Frame Forward F. Fast Forward G. Next Scene H. Button navigation arrows and Enter button I. Return to main menu J. Play Full Screen

To preview a menu-based DVD

You can preview a menu-based DVD at any point after dragging a DVD template onto the DVD Layout panel.

1 Click the Create DVD button ⦾, if necessary, to open the DVD Layout panel.

2 In the DVD Layout panel, click Preview DVD.

Note: If you are notified that buttons overlap, see "To change the placement and size of menu items" on page 201.

The Preview DVD window will open.

3 Use the navigation controls or your mouse to click each button and view each scene or video. If the menu or button thumbnails have video or audio, those clips play so that you can preview them before burning a DVD.

4 Click the Play Full Screen icon ▨ to preview the DVD full-screen.

5 Move the mouse. This will bring up a DVD control panel you can use, while in full-screen mode, to emulate the remote control for a DVD player.

For more information, see "Previewing a movie in the Monitor panel" on page 93.

Burning DVDs

About burning DVDs

Once you have previewed your DVD and are satisfied that it is complete, you are ready to burn the project to a DVD. Make sure that the DVD you've selected is compatible with both your DVD burner and DVD player. Also, you must have enough available hard disk space to accommodate the compressed DVD files as well as any scratch disk files created during export. If you don't have enough free disk space on one drive partition, you can specify a different partition for the scratch disk files using the Edit > Preferences > Scratch Disks command. (You can verify the space needed in the Burn DVD dialog box.)

Depending on the complexity and length of the project and your computer speed, compressing video and audio for a DVD can take hours. If you plan to burn multiple DVDs with the same content and quality, you can save time by burning them in the same session, which compresses the project only once.

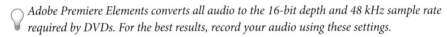 *Adobe Premiere Elements converts all audio to the 16-bit depth and 48 kHz sample rate required by DVDs. For the best results, record your audio using these settings.*

For more information, see "Guidelines for successful DVD burning" on page 210 and "Compatibility issues for DVDs" on page 209.

Supported DVD media

If a compatible DVD burner is connected to your computer, you can create a DVD directly from Adobe Premiere Elements. You can play the DVDs that you create in either a TV or computer DVD player. Adobe Premiere Elements creates DVDs that conform to DVD-video format. (It does not create data or audio DVDs.)

Adobe Premiere Elements supports single-layer, 4.7 GB discs of the following types: DVD+R, DVD+RW, DVD-R, and DVD-RW. It also supports dual-layer 8.5 GB DVD+R discs. Choose the media supported by both your DVD burner and the DVD player on which you plan to play the DVD. Not all DVD burners and DVD players support all types of DVDs. For example, many, but not all, TV DVD players recognize DVD+R discs.

DVD-R This format uses write-once recordable discs, and is compatible with both stand-alone DVD players and DVD-ROM drives. DVD-R discs are available in two media types: General Use and Authoring. Most consumer DVD-R burners use the cheaper General Use discs, and some professional burners use Authoring discs. You must use the correct media type for your burner. However, once written, the discs should be readable in either type of DVD player or drive. (General Use DVD-R is designed to prevent backup of encrypted commercial DVDs.)

DVD+R This non-rewritable format is compatible with most DVD players and DVD-ROM drives. The first generation +RW burners did not support DVD+R recording, and probably cannot be upgraded to do so. However, all current models of DVD+RW burners support DVD+R recording. Compatibility of DVD+R discs in stand-alone DVD players is similar to that of DVD-R.

DVD-RW/DVD+RW These formats are similar in functionality and compatibility with DVD burners and players. DVD-RW and DVD+RW use rewriteable discs that can rewrite more than 1000 times in ideal situations. The majority of stand-alone DVD players play video recorded on DVD-RW and DVD+RW discs, but the compatibility is not as high as with DVD-R and DVD+R. Current DVD-RW burners can also burn to DVD-R.

Note: If your DVD burner is not compatible with Adobe Premiere Elements, you can burn the project to a folder, which allows you to use the software included with the burner to burn the final DVD.

Compatibility issues for DVDs

When choosing DVD media and hardware, consider the following compatibility issues:

- The DVD+R and DVD-R formats are compatible with more set-top players than DVD+RW and DVD-RW.

- DVD-ROM drives are compatible with more DVD formats than set-top DVD players, often because computers can update firmware and drivers easier than a set-top player.

- Older DVD players support fewer DVD formats.

Video compression for DVDs

Making a DVD involves compressing your video into the MPEG-2 format. Compression reduces your video and audio files to take up less storage space. For example, a 60-minute video in Adobe Premiere Elements takes up approximately 13 GB. However, a single-layer DVD holds only 4.7 GB. (Dual-layer DVDs hold 8.5 GB.) To maintain maximum quality, Adobe Premiere Elements compresses the movie only as much as necessary to fit it on the DVD. The shorter your movie, the less compression required, and the higher the quality of the video on the DVD.

Compressing video and audio for use on a DVD is very time consuming, even on high-end, dedicated systems. The time required varies depending upon the speed of the computer processor, the amount of available memory, and the complexity and length of a project. A standard video project of 60 minutes may take from 4 to 6 hours to burn. Many DVD producers burn a project overnight.

Creating DVDs for different geographical regions

If you are sharing your DVD with someone from a different country, you may need to burn the DVD using a different TV standard. In most of the world, video devices (from camcorders to DVD players) conform to one of two TV standards: *NTSC* in Japan and North America, or *PAL* in most of Europe and the Middle East.

Adobe Premiere Elements can create both NTSC and PAL DVDs, so you can create DVDs appropriate for your region and other parts of the world. However, you get the best results if your captured video matches the TV standard to which you plan to export.

TV standard	Areas where commonly used	Frame size	Frames per second
NTSC	North America, parts of South America, Japan, the Philippines, Taiwan, South Korea, Guam, Myanmar, and others	720 x 480	29.97 fps
PAL	Europe, Middle East, and parts of the following continents: Asia, Africa, South America	720 x 576	25 fps

Guidelines for successful DVD burning

Once the movie includes the editing and navigation you want, the burning process is fairly straightforward. However, incompatible devices and media, or unexpected time factors can affect quality and completion. For a successful experience, consider the following guidelines when burning DVDs.

Note: If encoding errors occur, consult the Troubleshooting section in Help.

- Allow enough time. Compressing video and audio for a DVD can take hours. Consider burning the DVD overnight. If you plan to burn several DVDs, burn them in the same session by using the Copies option in the Burn DVD dialog box so that you compress the project only once. (See "Video compression for DVDs" on page 209.)

- Update drivers and firmware. Make sure that you have installed the latest drivers and *firmware* (software contained in a read-only device (ROM), which has instructions for controlling the operation of peripheral devices) for your DVD burner. You can download updates from the Internet.

- Choose a compatible DVD burner. To make a DVD in Adobe Premiere Elements, you must have a compatible DVD burner. First, make sure your system has a DVD burner, not just a CD-ROM, CD-R or DVD-ROM drive. Then, check to see if the drive is compatible with Adobe Premiere Elements by looking for it in the Burner Location menu of the Burn DVD dialog box. (See "To burn to a disc" on page 212.)

- Choose quality DVD recordable media and a compatible DVD media format. Not all DVD burners and DVD players support all types of DVDs. However, you can't burn the DVD unless your DVD burner supports the format of the disc. For example, a burner that supports only +R or +RW discs doesn't burn to -R or -RW discs. The same is true for DVD players. Many older DVD players might not recognize some rewritable discs created on a newer DVD burner. (See "Compatibility issues for DVDs" on page 209.)

- Provide plenty of defragmented, free hard disk space. You must have enough available hard disk space to accommodate the complete compressed DVD files, as well as any scratch files created during export. The space requirements for your project appear in the Burn DVD dialog box.

- Avoid making unnecessary DVD previews. Previews of your My Project panel are useful for checking how your finished movie looks and plays, but they take time to create and are not used in the DVD burning process.

- Test your DVDs. If you make a mistake with a recordable DVD, you must use another disc; whereas if you make a mistake with a rewritable DVD, you can reuse it. For this reason, consider using a DVD-RW (rewritable) disc for making test discs and then switching to a DVD-R General Use disc for final or extra copies. DVD-R for General Use is a write-once recordable format that provides excellent compatibility with both stand-alone DVD players and DVD-ROM drives.

- Avoid running nonessential computer tasks during export. Turn off screen savers and power savers. Avoid scanning for viruses, downloading updates, searching on the Web, playing computer games, and so on.

To burn to a disc

1 Before starting Adobe Premiere Elements, connect and turn on all external DVD burners.

2 In the DVD Layout panel, click Burn DVD.

You can also open the Burn DVD dialog box by selecting the My Project panel, and then choosing File > Export > Export To DVD.

3 In the Burn DVD dialog box, select Disc as the Burn To option.

4 Type a name for the DVD. This name appears in Windows if you insert the DVD into a computer. (The default name is a date stamp in 24-hour format: *YYYYMMDD_hhmmss.*)

5 Select a DVD burner for Burner Location.

6 Make sure that a compatible DVD is inserted in the drive. If you insert a disc, click Rescan to check all connected DVD burners for valid media.

7 In the Copies text box, enter the number of DVDs you want to burn during this session. You are prompted to insert new discs until all have been burned. Encoding the video and audio takes place only once.

8 Either select Fit Contents To Available Space or deselect that option and drag the slider to choose the video quality you want.

9 For Preset Selection, select the option for the television standard used in the geographic location of your audience.

10 Click Burn to begin converting your project to the DVD format and burning the DVD. If no DVD burner is available, you can burn to a folder, and then burn the VOB files to disc when the burner is available. (See "To burn to a DVD folder" on page 212.)

Important: Compressing the video and audio for DVD output can take several hours.

For more information, see "Compatibility issues for DVDs" on page 209 and "Guidelines for successful DVD burning" on page 210.

To burn to a DVD folder

If your DVD burner isn't compatible with Adobe Premiere Elements, you can burn the project to a folder instead. This creates a DVD-compatible file in MPEG-2 DVD format that can be burned to a DVD using a DVD authoring program such as Adobe Encore DVD.

1 If the DVD Layout panel is not displayed, click the Create DVD button .

2 In the DVD Layout panel, click Burn DVD.

3 In the Burn DVD dialog box, select one of the Folder options as your destination for the project. For movie projects bigger than a single-layer 4.7 GB, select Folder (8.5 GB), which can accommodate dual-layer discs.

4 Type a name for the folder.

5 Click Browse to specify a location for the DVD folder.

6 Click Burn to begin creating the DVD folder.

Important: *Compressing the video and audio for DVD output can take several hours.*

For more information, see "About archived projects" on page 229.

Chapter 13: Exporting and archiving

Exporting basics

File types available for export

The following file types are available when you export files using the File > Export commands or the Export button ![Export button icon]. Additional file types may be available with your video capture card or third-party plug-ins.

Video file types

- 3GP

- Animated GIF

- Filmstrip (.flm)

- Adobe Flash Video (.flv)

- Microsoft AVI (.avi)

- Microsoft DV AVI (.avi)

- MPEG-1 (Multimedia Compatible)

- MPEG-1 (VCD- and SVCD-compatible)

Note: Although Adobe Premiere Elements exports VCD- and SVCD-compatible MPEG files, you must use a VCD authoring program or a disc-burning program to burn those files to a CD.

- MPEG-2 (Multimedia Compatible .mpg)

- MPEG-2 (DVD-compatible .mpg)

- MPEG-2 (HDV .m2t: 1080i 25, 1080i 30, 720p 30)

- MPEG-4 (.mp4, .mov, .avi)

- QuickTime (.mov)

- Windows Media (.wmv)

Audio file types

- QuickTime (.mov)

- Microsoft AVI (.avi)

- Windows Waveform (.wav)

Note: *Though Adobe Premiere Elements can import Dolby AC-3 audio in a stand-alone .ac3 file with .vob (DVD) or .mod (SD-based camcorder) files, it exports the audio from it as Dolby Digital Stereo only.*

Still-image file types

- Adobe Title Designer (.prtl)

- GIF (.gif)

- JPEG (.jpg, .jpe, .jpeg, .jfif)

- TIFF (.tif, .tiff)

- Truevision Targa (.tga)

- Windows Bitmap (.bmp)

Sequence file types

- GIF sequence

- JPEG sequence

- Targa sequence

- TIFF sequence

- Windows Bitmap sequence

For more information, see "File types you can import" on page 66.

Exporting for hard disk playback

To export a movie for hard disk playback

The video you edit in the My Project panel is not available as an independent video file until you export it. After export, you can play it in other video playback or editing programs and move it to other disks or platforms. You can also export from the Preview window, and you can specify a range of frames to export.

Exporting a movie for hard disk playback generally creates files with data rates and file sizes that exceed the limits for successful Internet, VCD, SVCD, DVD, or handheld device playback.

⚲ *If you're having trouble exporting your movie to DVD, consider exporting it first as a stand-alone AVI or DV AVI file. Then place this single file into the My Project panel of a new project and export that to DVD. For more information, see the Troubleshooting section in Adobe Premiere Elements Help.*

1 Select the My Project panel and choose File > Export > Movie.

2 Click Settings, choose settings as necessary, and then click OK. (See "Export settings" in Adobe Premiere Elements Help.)

3 Specify a location and filename, and click Save. To cancel the export, press Esc; it may take several seconds to complete the cancellation.

⚲ *You can also export your video in DVD format to a folder on your hard drive.This is playable with some DVD player software. Click the Export button ▥. Then, choose To DVD, select the folder option, and specify a name and location for the folder. (See "To burn to a DVD folder" on page 212)*

To export a frame as a still image

You can export any frame or still-image clip as a still-image file. The frame is exported from the current time position in the Timeline view of the My Project panel or the Monitor panel. Following the export, the frame appears in the Available Media view of the Media panel.

1 Do one of the following:

• If using the Sceneline, drag the current-time indicator ⊤ in the Monitor panel to the frame you want to export.

- If using the Timeline, drag the current-time indicator 🦅 in the Timeline to the frame you want to export.

○ *For best results, pick a frame without too much motion.*

2 (Optional) Deinterlace the frame to greatly increase the quality of the exported image: In the Timeline, select the containing clip. Then choose Clip > Video Options > Frame Hold. Select Deinterlace and click OK.

○ *If Photoshop Elements is installed, you can instead deinterlace the exported image in that application. In the Editor, choose Filter > Video > Deinterlace.*

3 At the top of the Monitor panel, click the Freeze Frame button 📷 .

4 Click Export, choose settings as necessary, and then click OK. (See "Export settings" in Adobe Premiere Elements Help.)

5 Specify a location and filename, and click Save. To cancel the export, press Esc; it may take several seconds to complete the cancellation.

For more information, see "To freeze a video frame" on page 115 and "To export clips as a sequence of still images" on page 218.

To export clips as a sequence of still images

You can export a clip or movie as a sequence of still images, with each frame as a separate still-image file. Exporting as a sequence can be useful when you want to use a clip in an animation or 3D application that does not support video formats or requires a still-image sequence. When you export a still-image sequence, Adobe Premiere Elements numbers the files automatically.

1 Do one of the following:

- Select the My Project panel, and choose File > Export > Movie.
- In the Media panel, click the Available Media view button 🎞 . Then select a single clip and choose File > Export > Movie.

2 Click Settings.

3 For File Type, choose a still-image sequence format, such as JPEG, Targa, or TIFF. If you choose a movie format or animated GIF, all the frames will be in one file.

4 Choose the frames to export from the Range menu.

5 Click Video and specify options.

6 Click Keyframe and Rendering, specify options, and then click OK.

7 Specify a location for the exported still-image files. It's usually best to specify an empty folder set aside so that the sequence files don't become mixed with other files.

8 To set the sequence numbering, type a numbered filename. To specify the number of digits in the filename, determine how many digits will be required to number the frames, and then add any additional zeroes you want. For example, if you want to export 20 frames and you want the filename to have five digits, type **Car000** for the first filename (the remaining files will automatically be named Car00001, Car00002, ..., Car00020).

9 Click Save to export the still-image sequence.

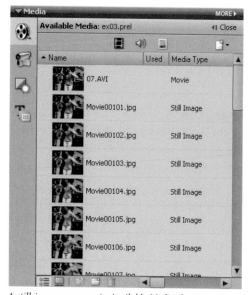

A still-image sequence in Available Media showing sequential numbering in filenames.

To export audio only

You can choose to export only the audio from your movie. Adobe Premiere Elements will save it in a Windows Waveform file (.wav).

Note: Adobe Premiere Elements can import, but not export MP3 files. Even if you have used MP3 files in your movie, you still must export its audio as a WAV file. You can then use a separate program, such as Adobe Audition, to convert this WAV file into an mp3.

1 Select the My Project panel and choose File > Export > Audio.

2 In the Export Audio dialog box, click Settings, choose settings as necessary, and then click OK.

3 Specify a location and filename, and click Save. To cancel the export, press Esc; it may take several seconds to complete the cancellation.

For more information, see "Export settings," and "To customize export settings" in Adobe Premiere Elements Help.

Exporting for the web and mobile devices

About web formats

Adobe Premiere Elements enables you to export your movie in formats suitable for delivery through the Internet or for use in iPods, PSP players, cell phones, or other mobile devices. In most cases, you select a format and preset, export the movie, and upload it to a host server. You can also customize and save presets for specific devices, servers, or audiences.

It is important to select a format supported by your web host, and Adobe Premiere Elements provides presets for each of these major formats:

- FLV (Adobe Flash Video) is a format commonly used to embed video into web pages and web applications.

- WMV (Windows Media) and MOV (QuickTime). These formats can play in either download-and-play or streaming modes. Streaming video is video that plays back as it downloads from the website, and typically does not need to be saved to your local hard drive.

- MPEG, MPEG-1, and MPEG-2 are commonly used for playback on discs, while MPEG-4 is often used on mobile devices and websites. The 3GP format for third-generation cell phones uses MPEG-4 video.

For more information, see "About compression," "About data rate," and "About compression keyframes" in Adobe Premiere Elements Help.

For more information, see "About burning DVDs" on page 208.

To export a movie for the web

When you are done editing your movie, you can simply choose one of the presets that Adobe Premiere Elements provides for export.

The provided presets cover the requirements of most servers and the bandwidth and player options available to most viewers. Using a provided preset is the quickest way to export your movie. You can also customize the settings to match a specific situation. Remember, however, to make sure that the data rate of your movie is appropriate for the intended playback medium.

1 Do one of the following:

- Click the Export button ▦, and choose one of the web-ready file formats listed: MPEG; Adobe Flash Video, Others; QuickTime; or Windows Media.

- Choose File > Export, and choose MPEG; Adobe Flash Video, Others; QuickTime; or Windows Media.

2 From the list on the left, select a preset that matches the data rate and television standard (NTSC or PAL) of your intended audience. The Preset Description section shows the default settings for each preset. The estimated properties of the movie appear in the Your Movie section. You can make adjustments to the default settings by clicking the Advanced button.

3 Click OK.

4 Specify a location and filename, and click Save.

Note: The first time you export with an MPEG 2 preset, the Activating Component dialog box may open. Follow the instructions to activate the MPEG2 component, and click OK. Component activation comes free of charge.

To export a movie for a mobile device

You can export movies for playback on cell phones, some PDAs, and portable media players, such as video iPods and PlayStation Portable (PSP) devices. Adobe Premiere Elements has presets that automatically provide for a number of these devices. You can also customize presets to match the format requirements of a given device.

Export using an iPod or PSP preset to produce your own video podcasts (also called vodcasts).

1 Consult the user guide for the device to determine the video file formats it supports.

2 With the My Project panel active, click the Export button ▦, and choose the file type (MPEG, Adobe Flash Video, Others, QuickTime, or Windows Media) supported by the device.

3 Do one of the following:

- For video iPods, cell phones, or PlayStation Portable devices, select an iPod, Mobile, or PSP preset from the Adobe Flash Video, Others presets.

- For MPEG devices, select a preset from the Multimedia Compatible presets.

- For QuickTime devices, select a preset from the For Wireless presets.

- For Windows Media devices, select an option from the For Wireless presets.

4 Click OK.

Note: The first time you export with an iPod, Mobile or PSP preset, the Activating Component dialog box opens. Follow the instructions to activate the H.264 component, and click OK. Component activation comes free of charge.

5 In the Save File dialog box, choose a location to save, and type a filename.

6 From the Export Range menu, choose either Entire Sequence or Work Area.

7 Click Save. Adobe Premiere Elements renders your movie into a file that you can copy to the device.

Note: You may need to customize a 3GP preset to export video that will play on a specific 3GP phone. Check your phone's user guide for its requirements. Also, not all phones support the 3GP format exported by Adobe Premiere Elements.

To customize options for web formats

Regardless of the file type you choose for export, the default settings for the corresponding video and audio options are adequate for most applications and produce high-quality results. However, you can change them if you have specific requirements not addressed by the default presets.

Important: Changing the Advanced settings without an in-depth understanding of video can produce undesirable results during playback.

When you change an option, you create a preset that you can name, save, and subsequently use in later projects. All presets that you create are listed in the Custom directory in the Export [*file format*] dialog box.

1 Click the Export button 🎬 and choose MPEG, Adobe Flash Video, Others, QuickTime, or Windows Media.

2 In the Export [*file format*] dialog box, click the Advanced button.

3 In the Export Settings dialog box, select Export Video, Export Audio, or both at the top of the dialog box to indicate which types of tracks to export.

4 Click the tab for the category that you want to adjust (Video, Audio, Multiplexer, Audiences, or Alternates), and adjust the corresponding options in the panel. The tabs and options displayed depend on the export type you chose.

5 After adjusting your options, click Save.

6 In the Choose Name dialog box, type a name for your preset and click OK.

7 In the Export [*file format*] dialog box, click Cancel.

Though it doesn't export a file at this step, Adobe Premiere Elements will apply your custom settings to subsequent exports.

For more information, see " "Video options for web formats," "Audio options for web formats" and "Alternates, and Audiences options" in Adobe Premiere Elements Help.

For more information, see "About web formats" on page 220.

To choose a saved export preset

Do one of the following:

• In the Export [*file format*] dialog box, expand the Custom folder and click a saved preset.

• In the Export Settings dialog box, choose a preset from the Presets menu.

Exporting to videotape

About exporting to videotape

Exporting your movie to tape is a good way to prepare it for easy presentation on TV screens, as well as a good way to archive it before removing it from your hard disk. Also, you can recapture the movies you have stored on tape and add them to new projects.

You can record your edited movie to tape from within Adobe Premiere Elements. If you are recording to a digital device, such as a DV camcorder, you can record video to it through your computer's IEEE 1394 port, conveniently controlling your camcorder's recording functionality from within Adobe Premiere Elements.

If you want to record to an analog device, such as a VCR or analog camcorder, you can record from Adobe Premiere Elements in either of these ways:

- Connect your analog device to a digitizing capture card or analog-to-digital converter (*AV DV converter*) which, in turn, is either installed into an expansion slot in your computer's motherboard or connected to it via one of its IEEE 1394 ports.

- Connect your analog device to the analog outputs of a digital device, such as a DV camcorder or deck. Connect the digital device to your computer, typically via their IEEE 1394 ports.

By using a third-party device controller, it is possible to use the device-control functionality of Adobe Premiere Elements with analog devices. Typically the device controller would connect to your computer via one of its serial ports and to your analog device through a LANC, control-S, Panasonic 5-pin (control-M), or RS-422 jack.

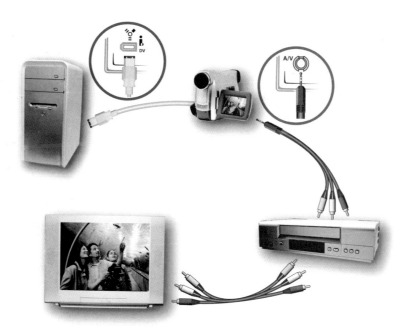

One way to connect an analog player to your computer

To export to tape with device control

If your recording device is connected to your computer by way of an IEEE 1394 port, or by way of a supported device controller, you can record your movie to tape using the export controls built into Adobe Premiere Elements.

1 Do one of the following:

- If your device has an IEEE 1394 port, connect it to the same type of port on your computer. Either of these will transmit both the video and the commands from the computer to the recording device.

- If your device has a LANC, Panasonic 5-pin (control-M), control-L, or RS422 jack, connect it to the same kind of jack on the device controller connected with your computer. This will transmit the computer's commands to your device. Also, connect your AV DV converter (or digital camcorder if you are using one to make the conversion) to your computer, and its analog audio and video outputs to your recording device.

2 Turn on the recording device and set it to VTR, VCR, or Play mode. If a dialog box appears, indicating that the Windows operating system just found the device you plugged in, close it.

3 Start Adobe Premiere Elements and open your project.

To give your recording device additional time before your video starts and after it ends, add black frames before and after the movie in the My Project panel. (See "To create and add a black video clip" in Adobe Premiere Elements Help.) In addition, if you plan to have a postproduction facility duplicate your videotapes, add a minimum of 30 seconds of color bars and tone at the beginning of your program to aid in video and audio calibration. (See "To add color bars and a 1-kHz tone" in Adobe Premiere Elements Help.)

4 Make sure that your recording device is on, that a blank or appendable tape is in the device, and that the tape's record protection tab is in a position that allows recording. If necessary, cue the tape to the location where you want to begin recording. Make sure that you have sufficient tape, and are recording at an optimal speed, in order to record your entire movie.

5 Click the Export button 🎬 and then choose To Tape.

6 In the Export To Tape dialog box, select options as desired. (See "Export To Tape options" on page 227.)

7 Click Record.

8 If the movie contains unrendered clips, the rendering begins at this point. Once all the clips are rendered, Adobe Premiere Elements sends a record command to your device and sends the movie to it.

9 When you are finished recording, click Stop and close the dialog box.

To export to tape without device control

If your device does not have an IEEE 1394 port and if you do not have a device controller for it, you can export a movie to it without using the device control functions built into Adobe Premiere Elements.

1 Connect your AV DV converter (or digital camcorder if you are using one to make the conversion) to your computer, and its analog audio and video outputs to your recording device.

2 If your device is a camcorder or if it is a deck with more than one set of inputs, set it to record audio and video signals through the inputs you desire.

3 Turn on the recording device and set it to the Record-Pause mode appropriate for the set of inputs you selected.

4 Start Adobe Premiere Elements and open your project.

5 If the movie contains unrendered clips, render them all.

6 Make sure that your video recording device is on, that a blank or appendable tape is in the device, and that the tape's record protection tab is in a position that allows recording. Cue the tape to the location where you want to begin recording. Make sure that you have sufficient tape, and are recording at an optimal speed, in order to record your entire movie.

7 Click the Export button ▥ and then choose To Tape.

8 In the Export To Tape dialog box, select options as desired. (See "Export To Tape options" on page 227.)

9 Put your device into its recording mode, and click Record.

10 When you are finished recording, click Stop and close the dialog box.

Export To Tape options

The following options are available in the Export To Tape dialog box. These options work only if you are recording to a DV camcorder that allows device control.

Activate Recording Device Lets Adobe Premiere Elements control your DV device.

Assemble At Timecode Indicates the place on your DV tape where you want the recording to begin, if you have a tape that already has timecode recorded, or striped, on it. You stripe a tape by first recording only black video before you record your footage. You record black video usually by recording with the lens cap on. If your tape is not striped, leave this option unselected to have recording begin at the location where you have cued the tape.

Delay Movie Start By n Quarter Frames Specifies the number of quarter frames that you want to delay the movie so that you can synchronize it with the DV device recording start time. Some devices need a delay between the time they receive the record command and the time the movie starts playing from the computer. Experiment with this setting if you are experiencing delays between the time you enable record and the time your DV device begins recording.

Preroll By n Frames Specifies the number of frames that you want Adobe Premiere Elements to back up on the recording deck before the specified timecode. Specify enough frames for the deck to reach a constant tape speed. For many decks, 5 seconds or 150 frames is sufficient.

Abort After n Dropped Frames Specifies the maximum number of dropped frames you want to allow before Adobe Premiere Elements aborts the recording. If you choose this option, you generally want to type a very low number because dropped frames will cause jerky playback and are indicative of a hard drive or transfer problem.

Report Dropped Frames Specifies that Adobe Premiere Elements displays the number of dropped frames.

Note: If you want to use device control but it's unavailable, click Cancel, choose Edit > Preferences, click Device Control, make sure that your device is set up properly in the Device Control options, and then click OK. Then try recording to tape again.

Exporting to Video CDs

About Video CD formats

You can store files in Video CD (VCD) format with a CD burner; a DVD burner isn't required. However, because of this format's smaller frame size and greater compression, it's quality is lower than that of VHS—much lower than DVD quality. The benefit of this lower quality is a smaller file size suitable for CDs, which can store only 700 MB.

Super Video CD (SVCD) format delivers greater picture resolution than VCD. Though SVCD files are larger files than VCD files, they are still much smaller than files in DVD format.

Most DVD players can play VCDs, but fewer can play SVCDs. However, most computers with CD-ROM drives and the appropriate software can play either type of video CD.

For more information, see "DVD basics" on page 187.

To export to Video CD or Super Video CD

You can create VCD and SVCD-compatible MPEG files by using the VCD Compatible and SVCD Compatible presets, respectively. Adobe Premiere Elements exports the MPEG file to the hard disk, but you must use a VCD authoring program to burn those files to a CD.

1 Click anywhere in the My Project panel to make it active.

2 Click the Export button 🎬, then choose MPEG.

3 In the MPEG dialog box, under SVCD Compatible or VCD Compatible, choose the television standard (NTSC or PAL) for the region in which the disc will be played. Then click OK.

4 In the Save File dialog box, specify a location to save to, type a filename, and choose either Entire Sequence or Work Area from the Export Range menu.

5 Click Save.

Adobe Premiere Elements saves the movie to a new VCD or SVCD MPEG file.

Note: *Adobe Premiere Elements will not burn the VCD or SVCD file to a CD. For that, you will need third-party software.*

For more information, see "About burning DVDs" on page 208 and "To burn to a disc" on page 212.

Archiving projects

About archived projects

The Project Archiver copies your project and its media to a folder for further editing or storage. You can use it to prepare an incomplete project for editing on another computer, to collect into one folder copies of media that may be located in several folders or drives, or to trim the media in a completed project down to only the parts you used before saving the project to an archive. The Project Archiver has two options, Archive Project and Copy Project. Since Copy Project does not trim the project, it often results in a folder containing more, and larger, files than does Archive Project.

Archive Project Creates a folder containing a new project file, and a new clip for each clip used in the original My Project panel at its edited length. The trimmed project includes up to 30 frames of extra footage, called *handles*, before the In point and after the Out point of each trimmed clip for minor adjustments you may want to make after archiving the project. A trimmed project excludes any rendered previews and audio previews (conformed audio), as well as any unused media. Adobe Premiere Elements automatically creates new audio previews (but not rendered previews) when you open the trimmed project. Clips in a trimmed project are renamed so that their filenames match the project filename. Use this option to ready a completed project for storage, before you remove it from your hard disk.

Note: *Project Archiver retains any effect keyframes and clip markers that exist beyond the In and Out points of a trimmed clip.*

Copy Project Creates a folder containing a new project file, and full copies of all the media that appear in the Available Media view of the Media panel in the original project, whether or not any of them were used in the My Project panel. Unlike Archive Project, Copy Project does save all rendered preview files. Use this option to aggregate copies of all files belonging to a project into a single folder. This easily can be transferred to another computer, or opened for further editing at a later time.

Archived project folders can be large, so archiving to a portable hard drive is recommended when you intend to transfer a project between computers. Using a disc-burning program, you can also burn trimmed or copied project folders to DVDs for archiving or transfer to other computers.

Project Archiver dialog box

To trim or copy a project

1 Choose File > Project Archiver.

2 In the Project Archiver dialog box, select either Archive Project to copy a trimmed version of your project or Copy Project to copy an untrimmed version, including all assets, to a new location.

3 To specify a folder for the project, click Browse and locate the folder. In the Browse For Folder dialog box, you can click Make Folder to create a new folder.

4 After you specify a folder, click OK, and then click OK again to close the Project Archiver dialog box.

Adobe Premiere Elements places the new files into a folder with a name that starts with either *Trimmed*, if you chose Archive Project, or *Copied*, if you chose Copy Project.

Chapter 14: Using Adobe Photoshop Elements with Adobe Premiere Elements

Using both products together

About the products

Adobe Photoshop Elements and Adobe Premiere Elements are designed to work together, whether you purchase the products separately or bundled in one package. These products seamlessly combine digital photography and video editing, letting you create exciting video projects.

Here are a few ways you can share files between Photoshop Elements and Adobe Premiere Elements:

- Organize your photos, video clips, and audio clips in Photoshop Elements, and then drag them into the Adobe Premiere Elements Media panel.

- Create a slide show in Photoshop Elements with captions, transitions, effects, music, narration, graphics, and titles, and then bring the slide show into Adobe Premiere Elements for further editing. Or, bring individual photos into Adobe Premiere Elements and create the slide show there.

- Customize DVD menu templates in Photoshop Elements, and then use them in your Adobe Premiere Elements project. (DVD templates are PSD files stored in the Adobe Premiere Elements application folder.)

- Create a Photoshop Elements file with your video project's settings, enhance it in Photoshop Elements, and then use it in Adobe Premiere Elements.

Arranging your work area

To share files between Photoshop Elements and Adobe Premiere Elements, it's useful to have both programs open and accessible on your computer monitor.

1 Start Photoshop Elements and Adobe Premiere Elements.

2 If your screen is maximized, click the Restore button ⬜ in the upper right corner of each application window.

3 Position the application windows side by side or overlap them slightly.

Getting files from Photoshop Elements

Differences in file type support

Photoshop Elements and Adobe Premiere Elements support many of the same file types, which makes the transfer of most files between the two programs easy and efficient. For example, you can catalog Photoshop (PSD) files in the Organizer and then add them as still images to a project in Adobe Premiere Elements.

However, the following file types are not recognized by both programs:

Supported by Photoshop Elements, but not Adobe Premiere Elements

- Adobe PDF (.pdf)

- TIFF with LZW compression (.tif)

Supported by Adobe Premiere Elements, but not Photoshop Elements

- MOD (.mod; JVC Everio)

Supported by Adobe Premiere Elements and the Editor, but not the Organizer

- Illustrator (.ai)

Supported by Adobe Premiere Elements and the Organizer, but not the Editor

- AIFF (.aiff)

- ASF (.asf)

- AVI movie (.avi; only partially supported)

Note: The Organizer catalogs video AVI files properly, but audio AVI files are shown as broken video thumbnail icons. However, they will play correctly.

- Dolby audio (.ac3)

- DVD (.vob)

- Flash video (.flv)

- MPEG (.mpg, .mp3, .mp4)

- QuickTime (.mov)

- WAV (.wav)

- Windows Media (.wmv, .wma)

The Editor can import individual video frames from ASF, AVI, MPEG, and Windows Media files. (Choose File > Import > Frame From Video.)

To access the Organizer from Premiere Elements

The Organizer in Photoshop Elements is a great place to gather the media files you use in your Premiere Elements projects.

1 In the Media panel of Premiere Elements, click the Get Media button .

2 Click Adobe Photoshop Elements to open the Organizer.

3 Add and organize media files for your video projects.

4 (Optional) To preview a video or audio file, double-click it. Then drag the position slider to the desired start point, and click the Play button .

To get files by dragging

You can drag files into the Adobe Premiere Elements Media panel, but not the My Project panel.

1 Make sure that both products are open and arranged so that you can see the Organizer in Photoshop Elements and the Media panel in Adobe Premiere Elements.

2 Select files in the Organizer. If you use the Photo Browser view, you can select more than one file by Ctrl-clicking each file that you want.

3 Drag the files into the Media panel.

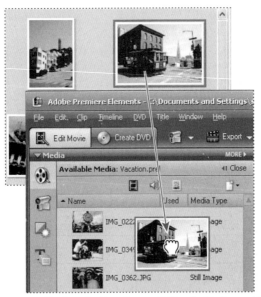

Dragging files from the Photo Browser (left) to the Media panel (right)

To get files by copying

You can paste files into the Adobe Premiere Elements Media panel, but not the My Project panel.

1 In the Photoshop Elements Organizer, select the files you want to paste into Adobe Premiere Elements. If you use the Photo Browser view, you can select more than one file by Ctrl-clicking each file that you want.

2 Choose Edit > Copy.

3 Switch to Adobe Premiere Elements and click the Media panel to make it active.

4 Choose Edit > Paste.

The files appear at the bottom of the Media panel.

To get files by using the Send To command

In the Photoshop Elements Organizer, the Send To Premiere Elements command adds selected files to the Media and My Project panels. This feature is useful for quickly incorporating a set of files into your video project, or for designing a visual layout of scenes (also referred to as a *storyboard*). Files are sent in the order they appear in the Organizer.

Note: *For best results, don't send audio files together with video and still-image files. Instead, copy or drag audio files to the Media panel in Adobe Premiere Elements. That way, you can add audio to a specific part of a movie.*

A storyboard collection in Photoshop Elements (top) used as an introduction to a movie in Adobe Premiere Elements (bottom)

1 In Adobe Premiere Elements, open a blank or existing project.

Note: *If you don't open the application first, Adobe Premiere Elements automatically opens a new blank project when you choose Send To Premiere Elements.*

2 In the Photoshop Elements Organizer, select the files you want to send to Adobe Premiere Elements. If you use the Photo Browser view, you can select more than one file by Ctrl-clicking each file that you want to send.

3 Choose File > Send To Premiere Elements.

Adobe Premiere Elements automatically adds the files to the Media panel and the end of the My Project panel. Still images appear in sequence using Adobe Premiere Elements defaults for clip duration and transition.

You can modify the default duration Adobe Premiere Elements uses when importing still images (for example, to create a faster paced slide show). Click the More button in the Media panel, and choose Still Image Duration. This change doesn't affect the duration of existing still images in a movie.

Enhancing slide shows with Premiere Elements

To add Photoshop Elements slide shows to video projects

Using Photoshop Elements, you can create a slide show of photos and enhance them with music, transitions, narration, text, and more. When you finish your creation, you can bring it into Adobe Premiere Elements and incorporate it into movies and DVDs.

Slide shows are connected in the two applications. After you add a slide show to a video project, any changes you make in Photoshop Elements automatically appear in Premiere Elements.

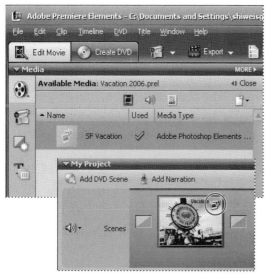

A slide show in the Media and My Project panels of Adobe Premiere Elements

1 In the Photoshop Elements Organizer, assemble and select photos for the slide show.

2 Click the Create button , and choose Slide Show.

3 In the Slide Show Preferences dialog box, set options such as default transitions and durations, and click OK.

4 Add music, narration, text, graphics, and so on. Then customize transitions and durations as needed.

5 To preview the slide show, click the Play button .

6 When you finish editing the slide show, click the Save Project button , enter a name, and click Save.

7 Click the Output button . Then select Send To Premiere Elements, and click OK.

If Premiere Elements is open, the slide show appears in the Media and My Project panels of the current project. If Premiere Elements is closed, it starts and prompts you to create a new project.

To edit slide shows in Adobe Premiere Elements

If you want to edit a slide show in Premiere Elements, break it apart so you can access individual components, such as images, text, and graphics.

Note: After you break apart a slide show, you can edit the resulting components only in Premiere Elements. Changes you make to the original slide show in Photoshop Elements will no longer appear in your video project.

Breaking apart a slide show

1 In the Sceneline of the My Project panel, right-click the slide show, and choose Break Apart Photoshop Elements Slide Show.

2 Edit the slide show in any of the following ways:

- To edit a transition, select it in the My Project panel, and adjust settings in the Properties panel.

- To replace a transition, click the Effects And Transitions button 🎬 in the Media panel. Then open the Video Transitions folder, and drag a new transition to the My Project panel.

- To extend or shorten a clip, select it in the My Project panel, and drag the In point 🔖 or Out point 🔖 in the Monitor panel.

- To change the size or position of text and graphics, select the containing clip in the My Project panel, and adjust text and graphics in the Monitor panel.

- To adjust the volume of narration or a soundtrack, select it in the My Project panel, and change settings in the Properties panel.

To burn a slide show to DVD

If Premiere Elements is installed, Photoshop Elements can burn a slide show directly to a high-quality DVD.

1 In Photoshop Elements, do one of the following:

- For a new slide show, choose File > Save As. Type a name and click Save.

- For an existing slide show, choose File > Save Slide Show Project. Type a name and click Save.

2 Choose File > Output Slide Show.

3 Click Burn To Disc.

4 Select the DVD option for the type of disc to burn.

5 Select the TV standard (NTSC or PAL) for the geographical region where the DVD will be played.

6 To include other slide show creations or WMV files on the disc, do the following:

- Select Include Additional Slide Shows I've Made On This Disc, and click OK.

- Click Add Slide Shows.

- Select the slide shows and click OK.

7 If you chose to include additional slide shows, do any of the following, and then click Next:

- To remove a slide show from the list, select it and click Remove Slide Show.

- To change the TV standard, select either NTSC or PAL in the Video Options area.

- To rearrange the slide shows on the DVD, drag their images to the positions you want.

8 Select a folder for the new files.

Photoshop Elements creates WMV files for each of the slide shows you included. (You can click Cancel in the progress dialog box at any time to stop the process.)

Adobe Premiere Elements adds the WMV files to its Media and My Project panels, and automatically opens the DVD workspace, where you select a menu template and add or customize menu buttons.

Enhancing videos with Adobe Photoshop Elements

To edit video frames in Photoshop Elements

If video frames need correction or enhancement in Photoshop Elements, use the Freeze Frame feature in Premiere Elements.

Editing a video frame in Photoshop Elements

1 In the Monitor panel of Premiere Elements, drag the current-time indicator to the frame you want to edit.

2 Click the Freeze Frame button .

3 To set Freeze Frame Duration, drag the Seconds value.

4 Select Edit in Photoshop Elements After Inserting, and then click Insert In Movie.

5 In the Photoshop Elements Editor, edit the image (apply filters, styles, effects, brush strokes, and so on).

Note: If you resize the image, it may become distorted in the video frame.

6 If you added image layers, choose Layer > Flatten Image.

7 When you finish making changes, choose File > Save.

8 Accept the default choices for file location and name, and click Save.

9 When Photoshop Elements reports that a file with the same name already exists, click OK to replace the file. Then click OK in the BMP Option dialog box.

Premiere Elements automatically updates the frame in your movie.

Creating Photoshop files in Adobe Premiere Elements

You can use Adobe Premiere Elements to open a new Photoshop (PSD) file in Photoshop Elements, with dimensions and aspect ratios equal to those of your project. (Photoshop Elements files and Photoshop files both use the PSD file name extension.) For example, if the Adobe Premiere Elements project is DV NTSC (720 x 480) with a pixel aspect ratio of 0.9, a template with the same specifications is used to create the PSD file. Creating a PSD file this way ensures that the file is optimized for your project. By default, the New > Photoshop File command in Adobe Premiere Elements places the new file in the Adobe Premiere Elements Media panel.

Having Adobe Premiere Elements manage the production of a still image in Photoshop Elements also eliminates any distortion during the video encoding of the image. Adobe Premiere Elements saves the image, properly scaled for display in video.

Once you create and save the file using Adobe Premiere Elements, you can go back to Photoshop Elements to edit the file. When you save and close the file in Photoshop Elements, it is automatically updated in Adobe Premiere Elements. You can also edit the file by using the Edit Original command in Adobe Premiere Elements.

Adobe Premiere Elements uses prebuilt templates as a basis for these PSD files. The templates are included in the Adobe Premiere Elements 3.0/Document Templates folder. You can create your own templates in Photoshop Elements and save them to the Document Templates folder if you want to create files of varying sizes in Photoshop Elements; however, they won't be preoptimized for your project.

To create a new Photoshop file

1 In Adobe Premiere Elements, choose File > New > Photoshop File.

2 Specify a location and name for the PSD file, and click Save.

The file opens in the Photoshop Elements Editor. If you selected Add To Project (Merged Layers), a black placeholder image also appears in the Adobe Premiere Elements Media panel.

3 In Photoshop Elements, edit the file, and then choose File > Save.

4 Specify options in the Save As dialog box and click Save.

The file appears in the Photoshop Elements Organizer and in the Adobe Premiere Elements Media panel.

Creating a Photoshop (PSD) file in Adobe Premiere Elements, optimized for your project.

Chapter 15: Keyboard shortcuts

Using default shortcuts

About keyboard shortcuts

For many tasks, using keyboard shortcuts is quicker than using a mouse. Adobe Premiere Elements provides a default set of keyboard shortcuts that you can view and modify by using the Edit > Keyboard Customization command.

To find the keyboard shortcut for a tool, button, or menu command

❖ Do one of the following:

- For a tool or button, hold the pointer over the tool or button until its tool tip appears. If a shortcut is available, it appears after the tool description.

- For menu commands, look for the keyboard shortcut at the right of the command.

- For keyboard shortcuts not shown in tool tips or menus, choose Edit > Keyboard Customization.

Customizing shortcuts

To create custom keyboard shortcuts

In addition to using the default set of keyboard shortcuts, you can assign your own custom shortcuts to nearly any menu command, button, or tool. You can save different sets of shortcuts and restore the default settings.

1 Choose Edit > Keyboard Customization.

2 In the Keyboard Shortcuts dialog box, choose an option from the pop-up menu:

- Application displays commands found in the menu bar, organized by category.

- Windows displays commands associated with window buttons and pop-up menus.

3 In the Command column, view the command for which you want to create a shortcut. If necessary, click the triangle next to the name of a category to reveal the commands it includes.

4 Click in the item's shortcut field to select it.

5 Do any of the following:

- To add a shortcut, type it.

Note: If the shortcut was used by another command, an alert appears at the bottom of the dialog box.

- To erase a shortcut, click Clear.

- To reverse either of the actions above, click Undo.

6 Repeat the procedure to enter as many shortcuts as you want. When you're finished, click Save As, type a name for your Key Set, and click Save.

Note: Some commands are reserved by the operating system and cannot be reassigned to Adobe Premiere Elements. Likewise, you cannot assign numbers or the plus (+) and minus (–) keys on the numeric keypad because they are necessary for entering relative timecode values. You can assign these keys on the keyboard, however.

To remove shortcuts

❖ In the Keyboard Customization dialog box, do one of the following:

- To remove a single shortcut, select it and click Clear.

- To remove a custom set of shortcuts, select the key set you want to remove from the Set pop-up menu and click Delete. When asked, confirm your choice by clicking Delete.

To switch to a different set of shortcuts

❖ Choose Edit > Keyboard Customization, and choose the set of shortcuts you want to use from the Set pop-up menu.

Index

Numerics

3GP 222

A

action-safe margins 157

Add DVD Scene tool 90

Add Marker tool 90

Add Narration tool 90

Add Text button

  See also Title Templates

  about 151

  creating titles with 152

Add To Project (Merged Layers) command 244

Add Tracks command 89

Adobe Flash Video 220

  export for web 221

Adobe Help Center

  about 2

  changing the view 6

  displaying More Resources 3

  Help topics in 3

  navigating Help 4

  preferences for 2

  printing Help topics 5

  searching Help topics 4

  viewing support documents 3

Adobe Illustrator

  file type 67

Adobe Photoshop

  file type 67

Adobe Photoshop Elements

  arranging work area with Adobe Premiere Elements 233

  editing video frames in 242

files, creating from Adobe Premiere Elements 244

installing 1

registering 1

removing 1

Adobe Premiere Elements

  1.0 projects, opening 40

  arranging work area with Photoshop Elements 234

  installing 1

  new features 8

  registering 1

  removing 1

  tutorials 11

Adobe Premiere Elements title

  adding file type 67

Adobe Press 7

Adobe Title Designer

  file type 215

AIFF file type 66

Animated GIF file type 215

animation

  about 143

  panels used for 144

animation. *See also Adobe Premiere Elements Help*

Archive Project option 229

arranging clips, about 79

aspect ratios

  See also Adobe Premiere Elements Help

attenuating audio 183, 185

audio

  adjusting input level (gain) 185

  CD, adding from 69

fade in or out 186

maintaining pitch 113

muting 186

playing for a clip 136

ripping 69

supported file types 66

track, tutorial about adding 22

volume, adjusting 183, 185

Audio Gain command 185

Audio Meters 184

audio mixing 183

audio tracks 89

Auto Save option 49

Auto-play DVDs

  about 187

  creating 198

  previewing 207

Auto-Save folder 49

Available Media

  Icon view 76

  List view 76

Available Media view

  of Media panel 44

AVI file type

  import 66

B

backgrounds

  video 203

backwards, playing. *See* reversing a clip

Bitmap file type 67, 215

bookmarks

  for Help topics 6

boosting audio 185

bounding box, for resizing menu items 201

Break Apart Photoshop Elements Slide Show command 240

Bring Forward 166

Bring To Front 166

burning DVDs

    guidelines 210

    slide shows 241

    steps 208

    supported media 208

    tutorial about 28

buttons. *See* menu buttons

C

camcorder, connecting 55

Capture panel 56

capture settings

    capturing to Timeline 61

Capture To Timeline option 61

capturing

    about 51

    device control 57

    DV camcorder, from 52

    DV tape, to 56

    extra frames 57

    from DVD camcorder 72

    preparing for 52

    scene detection 60

    system requirements 52

    Timeline, directly to 61

    tutorial about 35

cell phone import 51, 52, 66, 72

Center At Cut transition 123

    applying 121, 128

changes

    undoing 47

characters, selecting 158

clip 51

clip analysis tools. *See Adobe Premiere Elements Help*

clip markers. *See Adobe Premiere Elements Help*

clipping (distortion) 183, 184, 185

clips

    deleting 78

    fast motion 113

    freezing a frame 117

    naming 77

    previewing in Photoshop Elements 235

    reversing 115

    selecting 90

    slow motion 113

    splitting 109

    trimming 99, 102

    tutorial about assembling 12

    volume 183

Compact view, in Adobe Help Center 6

Compact view, of tutorials 7

compatibility

    Adobe Premiere Elements 1.0 40

    DVD discs 208, 209

Component Activation 221, 222

compression. *See Adobe Premiere Elements Help*

Compuserve GIF file type 67

Constant Gain audio transition 122, 123

Constant Power audio transition 122, 123

context menus 43, 46

Copy Project option 229

crashes, using AutoSave to recover from 49

crawling titles 174, 175, 176

Create DVD button 188

crossfade 186

current-time indicator

    positioning the Timeline 92

    Timeline 91

D

data rate. *See Adobe Premiere Elements Help*

data transfer rate 52

deinterlacing

    freeze frames 117

deleting clips 84

device control 57

digital cameras, photos from 52

digital video. *See* DV

discs, for DVDs 208

distortion, in audio 183

distributing objects 167

Dolby AC-3 file type 66

downloading updates, plug-ins, and tryouts 8

dragging files from Photoshop Elements to Adobe Premiere Elements 235

drop shadows 174

dropped frames, preventing 55

dual-layer discs 208

duration

    default for importing still images 238

    transition 129

DV

capture, preparing for 55

tape, recording to 224

DV camcorders, adding files from. *See also* capturing

DVD burning. *See* burning DVDs

DVD camcorders, adding files from 72

DVD file type 215

DVD formats

auto-play 198

types of 187

DVD markers

about 188

adding 191, 193

deleting 197

finding 196

Main Menu Markers 189

naming 193, 196

Scene Markers 190

Stop Markers 188

tutorial about 28

DVD menu buttons. *See* menu buttons

DVD menus. *See* menus

DVD scene markers 81

DVD Templates

view of Media Panel 44

DVD workspace 39, 43, 45

DVDs

checking media 212

compressing 209

previewing 207

E

Edit workspace 39, 43, 45

Editor

defined 233

effect presets

about 138

applying 139

locating 132

effects

about 131

adjusting 139, 140

animating 143

applying and previewing 134

copying and pasting 136

gallery. *See Adobe Premiere Elements Help*

locating 132, 133

presets 132

removing 137

resetting 141

standard and fixed 131

tutorial about 18

Effects And Transitions panel 132

Effects and Transitions view of Media panel 44

Effects Controls window. *See* Properties panel

Enable command 183

Encapsulated PostScript file type 67

End At Cut transition 123

applying 121, 128

export

title 151

exporting

audio 219

clip as still image 218

frame as still image 217

hard disk playback, for 217

movies for the web 222

videotape, to 224, 226

work area 217

exporting. *See Adobe Premiere Elements Help*

F

fades, creating 146

fast motion 113

features

new 8

file formats 234

file sharing

between Photoshop Elements and Adobe Premiere Elements 235

dragging between programs 238

sending from Adobe Premiere Elements to Photoshop Elements 237

file types, supported 66, 215

files

audio, adding 68

still images, adding 69

supported 66

video, adding 67

Filmstrip (FLM) file type 66

Filmstrip file type 215

fixed effects 131

FLV format 220

folders

archived projects, for 229

fonts 151

changing 158

specifying 160

formats. *See* file types

forums 7

Frame Hold command 117

frames
  editing in Photoshop
    Elements 242
  exporting as still images 217
  freezing 117
  holding 117
freeze frame
  about 115
  creating 115
Full Screen Preview command 238
Full view, in Adobe Help Center 6
full-screen preview 95, 96, 97
  controlling 97
  to exit 97

G

gain
  normalizing 186
  optimizing 186
Get Media From view
  of Media panel 44
GIF file type 215
Go To DVD Marker
    command 196
guidelines
  burning DVDs 210

H

handles
  capturing 57
HDV projects 42
Help system
  about 3
  navigating 4
  printing from 5
  searching 4
  updating topics 2

Help system, tutorials in 7
History panel 47, 48
holding a frame 115
How To panel 46
  to open 46

I

Icon file type 67
IEEE 1394
  capture, preparing for 52
  connecting camcorder to
    computer 55
Image Control effect 131
image stills. *See* still images
importing
  about 51
  file types for 66
  non-DV devices, from 72
In and Out points
  about 99
  retrieving trimmed 111
  setting in Monitor panel 102
  setting in Timeline 105
Info panel 46
Insert edit. *See* Split and Insert
installing
  instructions for 1
interlacing. *See* Adobe Premiere
    Elements Help
Internet, creating video for 220
interpolation
  about 143
iPod 220
  export for 221

J

JPEG file type 67, 215
Justify command 160

K

keyboard shortcuts 245
keyframe area 145
keyframes
  about 143
  adding 144, 146
  controls for 143
  displaying 146
  editing 144
  guidelines 144
  removing 147
  specifying values for 148
  summary 146
  values, specifying 148

L

linked clips
  *See also Adobe Premiere
    Elements Help*
linking
  menu buttons 188, 189

M

Macintosh PICT file type 67
Main Menu Markers
  about 188, 189
  adding 193
  deleting 197
  renaming 196
markers
  See also DVD markers
Media Downloader 72

Media panel 44
about 43, 75
Available Media view of 44
deleting items 78
DVD Templates view 44
Effects and Transitions view 44
finding items 77
Get Media From view 44
Title Templates view 44
viewing items 76
memory sticks, adding files from 72
menu buttons
animating 195, 205
deleting 202
linking 188, 189
thumbnails 194, 196
menu templates. *See* templates
menu-based DVD
about 187
previewing 207
menus
See also menu buttons
audio and video, adding 203
creating 198
customizing 199
editing 201, 202
panels, in 46
scene markers, adding 191
templates 199
Microsoft AVI file types 215
mini-timeline
in the Monitor panel 94
in the Preview window 102
mistakes, undoing 47
mixing audio 183
mobile devices 221

mobile phone import 51, 52, 66, 72
mobile phones, adding files from 72
Monitor panel 93, 95, 96
about 43
playback controls 93
retrieving frames 111
trimming 102
More button 46
motion
menus 203
Motion effect
about 131
animating 144
Motion Menu Button option 195, 205
MOV format 220
Movie command 218
movies
rendering 93
tutorial about assembling 12
moving clips
in the Sceneline 83
mp3 file type 66
MPEG file type 66
MPEG formats, choosing 220
MPEG-1 file type 215
MPEG-2
component activation 221
compression 209
file type 215
MPEG2
component activation 68
muting audio 183
My Project panel 44, 79
Sceneline view of 81
Timeline view of 88

N
narration
record 180
replace or discard 181
set up for 179
Narration track 81, 180
new features 8
New Project command 39
normalizing gain 186
NTSC
TV standard 210
NTSC projects 42

O
objects
adjusting opacity 168
adjusting position 168
aligning 167
creating shadows 174
distributing 168
rotating 169
scaling 169
transforming 168
onion skinning
about 62
seeing 63
online Help 3
online training 7
Opacity effect 131
Open Project command 40
Organizer
defined 233
overscan, on TV sets 157

P
PAL projects 42
PAL, TV standard 210

palettes. *See* panels

panels

    about 43

    menus in 43, 46

PCX file type 67

Photoshop Elements. *See* Adobe
    Photoshop Elements

Photoshop. *See* Adobe Photoshop

PICT file type 67

Picture In Picture overlays

    creating 84

    deleting 86

Picture-in-Picture (PiP)
    presets 138

Play Full Screen 95, 96

Play/Pause button 93

playback

    speed, changing 90

plug-ins

    in Adobe Store 8

podcast 221

Portable Network Graphic file
    type 67

Premiere Elements. *See* Adobe
    Premiere Elements

presets

    See also Adobe Premiere
        Elements Help

    See also effect presets and
        project presets

    effects 138, 139

    included with Adobe Premiere
        Elements 132

preview files. *See Adobe Premiere*
    Elements Help

Preview Monitor. *See* Preview
    window

Preview window 100

previewing

    DVDs 207

    full-screen 96

    methods of 95

    movies 93

    slide shows 238

    video clips in Photoshop
        Elements 235

previews, in copied projects 229

printing

    Help topics 5

Project Archiver command 229,
    231

project presets

    about 41

    changing 42

    choosing 41

    custom or third-party 42

    HDV 42

    location of 42

    NTSC 42

    PAL 42

    widescreen 42

project settings

    about 41

    custom 41

    default 41

    presets 42

    reviewing 43

projects

    about 39

    archiving 229

    backing up and recovering 49

    moving 229

    opening 40

    saving 48, 49

    settings for 41

starting 39

    trimming 231

Properties panel 44

    adjusting properties 139

    keyframing 144, 148

PSD files

    adding to video projects 244

    creating from Adobe Premiere
        Elements 243

    opening in Adobe Premiere
        Elements 243

Q

QuickTime

    file type 215, 220

QuickTime file type 66

R

Razor At Current Time Indicator
    command 109

Razor tool 109

recording to tape 224, 227

redoing changes 47

registering

    instructions for 1

remotely controlling a
    camcorder 57

removable media, adding files
    from 72

removing middle frames from a
    clip 103

renaming

    clips 77

    source files 77

render

    preview 98

    set area 97

Render Work Area command 93

rendering, about 93

repeated frames, in transitions 119, 121, 123

Rescan command 212

resizing menu items 201

Reveal Marker In Timeline option 196

reversing a clip 115

reversing video 115

ripping audio 69

rolling titles 174, 175, 176

rough cut, creating 79

RSS feeds 3

S

Safe Action margin 157

safe margins

See also Adobe Premiere Elements Help

about 157

displaying and hiding 158

resizing 158

Safe Title margin 157

Save A Copy command 48

Save As command 48

Save command 48

Scene Detect 60

Scene Markers

See also DVD markers

about 188, 190

adding 191, 193

deleting 197

renaming 196

Sceneline 79, 81

about 81

deleting clips in the 84

to insert a clip before another in 82

to move a clip in 83

to place a clip in 82

view of My Project panel 44

scratch disks. See Adobe Premiere Elements Help

selecting

clips 90

text 158

Selection tool 90

Send Backward 166

Send To Back 166

Send To Premiere Elements command 237

sequence file types, supported 215

Set In button 102

Set Out button 102

settings

project 42

shadows, in titles 174

sharing files

between Photoshop Elements and Adobe Premiere Elements 233, 236

examples 233

Slide Show Preferences dialog box 238

slide shows

burning to DVD 241

customizing for video 238

editing in Adobe Premiere Elements 240

scene markers 191

tutorial about 17

slideshows

creating 86

expanding or closing grouped 87

grouped 86, 87

slow motion 113

software

downloads 8

registering 1

updating 2

soundtrack

adding a 182

previewing a 182

Soundtrack track 81, 182

soundtracks. See tracks

source clips

deleting 78

locating 40, 77

specialty clips. See Adobe Premiere Elements Help

Split And Insert 83

splitting clips

about 109

square-pixel footage. See Adobe Premiere Elements Help

stacking order 166

Start At Cut transition 123

applying 121, 128

still frames, in menu buttons 194

Still Image Duration command 238

still images

adding 69

creating from Adobe Premiere Elements 244

duration 71

exporting 217

menu buttons, in 194

modifying default duration 238

project size 70

scene markers 191

sending to Adobe Premiere Elements 237

supported file types 66, 69

Stop Markers
about 188
adding 193, 195
deleting 197
stop-motion capture
about 61
capturing from live source 62
deleting frames 64
playback settings 62
preferences 62
previewing 65
set up for 61
Time Lapse mode 63
storyboard 81
storyboard. *See* Sceneline
styles, for titles 162
summary keyframes 146
support documents, in Adobe
Help Center 3
support options 6
See also Help
system requirements
about 1

T
Targa file type
export 215
import 67
task bar 39
technical support
See also Help
complimentary and paid 6
on Adobe.com 7
television standards. *See* TV,
standards

templates
about 188, 198
buttons, deleting 202
choosing 199
text
selecting in titles 158
Thumbnail Offset timecode 194
thumbnails
buttons, selecting for 194
TIFF file type 67, 215
Time Lapse 61, 63
time ruler
in Properties panel 139
matching to In and Out
points 145
Timeline, in 88
zooming in or out 92
Time Stretch command 113, 115
Time Stretch tool 90, 113
timecode 91
about 65
display in Capture panel 65
recording at specific 227
time-lapse capture
set up for 61
Timeline 79
about 88
capturing to 61
creating keyframes 144
keyframe editing 144
moving through 91
retrieving frames 111
tools in the 90
tracks, adding 89
trimming 105
view of My Project panel 44

timeline markers. *See Adobe
Premiere Elements Help*
title instance
trimming a 154
title styles 162
Title Templates 155
Title Templates view
of Media panel 44
Titler.*See* Add Text button
titles
about 151
adding images 165
adding images to text boxes 165
adding shapes 164
animating 174
crawling 174
creating from templates 156
deleting styles 163
exporting 151, 176
for TV sets 157
importing 177
previewing on a TV 156
renaming styles 163
rolling 174
safe margins 157
saving styles 162, 163
setting styles 163
stacking order 166
still 152
templates for 155
text in 158, 160
trimming 154
title-safe margins 157
tools
editing 90

tracks
   adding and deleting 89
   naming 89
tracks, video and audio 89
training resources 6, 7
transitions
   about 119
   aligning 122, 123, 129
   applying 121
   default 127
   double-sided 121, 123
   duration 129
   locating 120
   previewing 122, 123
   repeated frames 119
   replacing 128
   single-sided 121
   storing favorites 127
   tutorial about 18
trimming
   about 99
   in Monitor panel 102
   in Timeline 105
   projects 231
   retrieving frames from 111
   titles 154
troubleshooting. *See Adobe
      Premiere Elements Help*
Truevision Targa file type
   export 215
   import 67
tryouts 8
tutorials, in Help 11
TV
   previewing titles on 156
TV standards 210

U
undoing changes 47
updates 8
updating
   software and Help topics 2
USB 2.0
   about 56
   video capture 52
user forums 7

V
VHS tape, recording to 224
video
   files, adding 67
   menu buttons, in 195, 205
   supported file types 66
video clips. *See* clips
video frames. *See* frames
video tracks 89
videotape
   capturing from 56
   exporting to 224, 226
views
   in Adobe Help Center 6
vodcast 221
voiceover. *See* narration
Volume effect 131
volume level 183, 185

W
web-ready movies 220
web-ready movies. *See Adobe
      Premiere Elements Help*
widescreen project, preset for 42
Windows Bitmap file type 215
Windows Media file type 66, 215
Windows WAVE file type 66, 215

WMV format 220, 241
work area bar 93, 94
workflow, tutorial 11
workspaces
   about 39, 43
   arranging for multiple
      applications 233
   choosing 45
   customizing 43
   DVD 43, 45
   edit 43, 45

Z
zooming
   Timeline, in 88, 92